Lecture Notes in Computer Science 13711

More information about this series at https://link.springer.com/bookseries/558

Mike Papadakis · Silvia Regina Vergilio (Eds.)

Search-Based Software Engineering

14th International Symposium, SSBSE 2022
Singapore, November 17–18, 2022
Proceedings

Editors
Mike Papadakis ⓘ
Université du Luxembourg
Luxembourg, Luxembourg

Silvia Regina Vergilio ⓘ
Federal University of Paraná
Curitiba, Brazil

ISSN 0302-9743   ISSN 1611-3349 (electronic)
Lecture Notes in Computer Science
ISBN 978-3-031-21250-5   ISBN 978-3-031-21251-2 (eBook)
https://doi.org/10.1007/978-3-031-21251-2

This Springer imprint is published by the registered company Springer Nature Switzerland AG
The registered company address is: Gewerbestrasse 11, 6330 Cham, Switzerland

Preface

Message from the General Chair

I would like to welcome all readers to the proceedings of the 14th edition of International Symposium on Search Based Software Engineering (SSBSE 2022). SSBSE continues to be the premier venue for researchers and practitioners who are interested in the application of automated search techniques for challenging software engineering problems. The 2022 edition of the symposium also marked its first return to a physical event after the global pandemic during 2020 and 2021, being collocated with ESEC/FSE in Singapore. However, considering the situations in many different parts of the world, SSBSE 2022 was also hybrid: in addition to making all presentations available online, it had a whole second day that took place online.

This complicated arrangement would not have been possible without the dedication from the organization committee. I would like to thank Michail and Silvia, who worked very hard to compile the excellent research track program. I also thank Marcio and Jeongju, who led the Replications and Negative Results (RENE) track as well as the New Ideas and Emerging Results (NIER) track, and Robert Feldt for the Journal First track. I thank Giovanni, Gunel, and Thomas for working hard to run the Challenge track. José and Chaima did an excellent job of maintaining the symposium's online presence, while Gabin provided impeccable web support.

Very special thanks go to our sponsors, Meta and the Korea Advanced Institute of Science and Technology (KAIST). Finally, I would like to thank Vivy Suhendra at the National University of Singapore for her support as the conference chair of ESEC/FSE 2022 - I do not know whether this collocation would have been possible without your help.

November 2022

Shin Yoo

Preface

Message from the Program Chairs

On behalf of the SSBSE 2022 Program Committee, it is our pleasure to present the proceedings of the 14th International Symposium on Search-Based Software Engineering. Search-Based Software Engineering (SBSE) is a research area focused on the formulation of software engineering problems as search problems, and the subsequent use of complex heuristic techniques to attain optimal solutions to such problems. A wealth of engineering challenges – from test generation to design refactoring and process organization – can be solved efficiently through the application of automated optimization techniques. SBSE is a growing field – sitting at the crossroads between AI, machine learning, and software engineering – and SBSE techniques have begun to attain human-competitive results. SSBSE 2022 continued the strong tradition of bringing together the international SBSE community in an annual event to discuss and to celebrate progress in the field.

This year, SSBSE had a total of 15 valid submissions in all tracks. We would like to thank all authors and reviewers for their efforts in making the conference program interesting and broad. Specifically, we received 11 papers to the Research track, one paper to the Challenge track, and three to the RENE/NIER track. At the end of the double-blind review process, where each submitted paper was reviewed by at least three SBSE researchers, six papers were accepted to the Research track and one paper was accepted to the Challenge track and the RENE/NIER tracks.

The program included two keynote talks, one from Lionel Briand, who reported his experiences and lessons learned in applying search-based solutions to test and analyze ML-enabled systems, and one from Justyna Petke, who reported her experience and research in genetically improving software systems. Additionally, the program also included a tutorial on guidelines for evaluating multi-objective SBSE approaches from Miqing Li and Tao Chen. Finally, the SSBSE community had the opportunity to discuss the future of the Search-Based Software Engineering area with outstanding researchers from the field.

We would like to thank the members of the SSBSE 2022 Program Committee. Their continuing support was essential to further improve the quality of accepted submissions and for the resulting success of the conference. Finally, the symposium would not have been possible without the efforts of the Organizing Committee, which we would like to thank. Particularly, we would like to thank:

– General Chair: Shin Yoo
– Journal First Track Chair: Robert Feldt
– NIER and RENE Track Co-chairs: Márcio Barros and Jeongju Sohn
– Challenge Track Co-chairs: Giovani Guizzo, Gunel Jahangirova and Thomas Vogel
– Publicity Co-chairs: Chaima Boufaied and José Miguel Rojas
– Web Chair: Gabin An

We hope you will find the work presented in this volume interesting and enjoyable.

November 2022   Mike Papadakis
                                                   Silvia Regina Vergilio

Organization

General Chair

Shin Yoo   KAIST, South Korea

Program Committee Chairs

Mike Papadakis   University of Luxembourg, Luxembourg
Silvia Regina Vergilio   Federal University of Paraná, Brazil

Journal First Track Chair

Robert Feldt   Chalmers University of Technology/University of
                                  Gothenburg, Sweden

NIER and RENE Tracks Chairs

Márcio Barros   UNIRIO, Brazil
Jeongju Sohn   University of Luxembourg, Luxembourg

Challenge Track Chairs

Giovanni Guizo   University College London, UK
Gunel Jahangirova   USI Lugano, Switzerland
Thomas Vogel   Paderborn University/Humboldt-Universität zu
                                  Berlin, Germany

Publicity Chairs

Chaima Boufaied   University of Ottawa, Canada
José Miguel Rojas   University of Sheffield, UK

Web Chair

Gabin An   KAIST, South Korea

Steering Committee

Shaukat Ali	Simula Research Laboratory, Norway
Gregory Gay	Chalmers University of Technology/University of Gothenburg, Sweden
Phil McMinn	University of Sheffield, UK
Mike Papadakis	University of Luxembourg, Luxembourg
Federica Sarro	University College London, UK
Shin Yoo	KAIST, South Korea

Program Committee

Aldeida Aleti	Monash University, Australia
Shaukat Ali	Simula Research Laboratory, Norway
Paolo Arcaini	National Institute of Informatics, Japan
Márcio Barros	UNIRIO, Brazil
Matteo Biagiola	Universitá della Svizzera italiana, Italy
Thelma E. Colanzi Lopez	State University of Maringá, Brazil
Pouria Derakhshanfar	Delft University of Technology, Netherlands
Xavier Devroey	University of Namur, Belgium
Thiago Ferreira	University of Michigan - Flint, USA
Alessio Gambi	IMC University of Applied Sciences Krems, Austria
Lars Grunske	Humboldt-Universität zu Berlin, Germany
Giovani Guizzo	University College London, UK
Fuyuki Ishikawa	National Institute of Informatics, Japan
Gunel Jahangirova	USI Lugano, Switzerland
Claire Le Goues	Carnegie Mellon University, USA
Inmaculada Medina-Bulo	Universidad de Cádiz, Spain
Leandro Minku	University of Birmingham, UK
Manuel Núñez	Universidad Complutense de Madrid, Spain
Mitchell Olsthoorn	Delft University of Technology, Netherlands
Annibale Panichella	Delft University of Technology, Netherlands
José Miguel Rojas	University of Sheffield, UK
Federica Sarro	University College London, UK
Jeongju Sohn	University of Luxembourg, Luxembourg
Valerio Terragni	University of Auckland, New Zealand
Thomas Vogel	Paderborn University/Humboldt-Universität zu Berlin, Germany

NIER and RENE Tracks Committee

Carlos Cetina	San Jorge University, Spain
Gregory Gay	Chalmers University of Technology/University of Gothenburg, Sweden
Emanuele Iannone	University of Salerno, Italy
Bruno Lima	University of Porto/INESC TEC, Portugal
Pasqualina Potena	RISE Research Institutes of Sweden AB, Sweden
Fabiano Pecorelli	Tampere University, Finland
José Raúl Romero	University of Cordoba, Spain
Chaiyong Ragkhitwetsagul	Mahidol University, Thailand
Jeongju Sohn	University of Luxembourg, Luxembourg
Andrea Stocco	Università della Svizzera italiana, Switzerland
Fiorella Zampetti	University of Sannio, Italy

Challenge Track Committee

Aldeida Aleti	Monash University, Australia
Wesley Assunção	Johannes Kepler University Linz, Austria
Jose Campos	University of Lisbon, Portugal
Tao Chen	Loughborough University, UK
Thelma E. Colanzi Lopez	State University of Maringá, Brazil
Erik Fredericks	Grand Valley State University, USA
Gregory Gay	Chalmers University of Technology/University of Gothenburg, Sweden
Gregory Kapfhammer	Allegheny College, USA
Stephan Lukasczyk	University of Passau, Germany
Inmaculada Medina-Bulo	Universidad de Cádiz, Spain
Manish Motwani	University of Massachusetts, USA
Rebecca Moussa	University College London, UK
Pasqualina Potena	RISE Research Institutes of Sweden AB, Sweden
José Miguel Rojas	University of Sheffield, UK

Sponsoring Institutions

Meta Platforms, Inc. USA
KAIST South Korea

Keynotes

Applications of Search-based Software Testing to Trustworthy Artificial Intelligence

Lionel C. Briand

University of Ottawa and University of Luxembourg

Abstract. Increasingly, many systems, including critical ones, rely on machine learning (ML) components to achieve autonomy or adaptiveness. Such components, having no specifications or source code, impact the way we develop but also verify such systems. This talk will report on experiences and lessons learned in applying search-based solutions to test and analyse such ML-enabled systems. Indeed, our results have shown that metaheuristic search plays a key role in enabling the effective test automation of ML models and the systems they are integrated into. Though other techniques are also required to achieve scalability and enable safety analysis, for example, the black-box nature of ML components naturally lends itself to search-based solutions.

Genetic Improvement of Software

Justyna Petke

University College London

Abstract. Genetic improvement uses computational search to improve existing software with respect to a user-defined objective function, while retaining some existing behaviour, usually captured by testing. Work on genetic improvement has already resulted in several awards. GI has been used, for instance, to automate the process of program repair, to speed up software for a particular domain, and to minimize memory and energy consumption. GI has also been used to transplant functionality from one software to another in an automated way. I will give an overview of the genetic improvement area and present key components of a GI framework.

Tutorial

Methodology and Guidelines for Evaluating Multi-Objective Search-Based Software Engineering

Miqing Li[1] and Tao Chen[2]

[1] University of Birmingham
[2] Loughborough University

Abstract. Search-Based Software Engineering (SBSE) has been becoming an increasingly important research paradigm for automating and solving different software engineering tasks. When the considered tasks have more than one objective/criterion to be optimised, they are called multi-objective ones. In such a scenario, the outcome is typically a set of incomparable solutions (i.e., being Pareto non- dominated to each other), and then a common question faced by many SBSE practitioners is: how to evaluate the obtained sets by using the right methods and indicators in the SBSE context? In this tutorial, we seek to provide a systematic methodology and guide- line for answering this question. We start off by discussing why we need formal evaluation methods/indicators for multi-objective optimisation problems in general, and the result of a survey on how they have been dominantly used in SBSE. This is then followed by a detailed introduction of representative evaluation methods and quality indicators used in SBSE, including their behaviors and preferences. In the meantime, we demonstrate the patterns and examples of potentially misleading usages/choices of evaluation methods and quality indicators from the SBSE community, high-lighting their consequences. Afterwards, we present a systematic methodology that can guide the selection and use of evaluation methods and quality indicators for a given SBSE problem in general, together with pointers that we hope to spark dialogues about some future directions on this important research topic for SBSE. Lastly, we showcase several real-world multi-objective SBSE case studies, in which we demonstrate the consequences of incorrect use of evaluation methods/indicators and exemplify the implementation of the guidance provided.

Contents

Research Papers

Search-Based Test Suite Generation for Rust

Vsevolod Tymofyeyev and Gordon Fraser[(✉)]

University of Passau, Passau, Germany
Gordon.Fraser@uni-passau.de

Abstract. Rust is a robust programming language which promises safety and performance at the same time. Despite its young age, it has already convinced many and has been one of the most popular programming languages among developers since its first release. However, like any other software, Rust programs need to be tested extensively. In this work, we propose the first search-based tool, called RUSTYUNIT, for automatic generation of unit tests for Rust programs. RUSTYUNIT incorporates a compiler wrapper, which statically analyzes and instruments a given program to generate and evaluate tests targeting high code coverage using a many-objective genetic algorithm. An initial empirical study using 6 real-world open-source Rust libraries demonstrates the feasibility of our approach but also highlights important differences and open challenges for test generation for Rust programs.

Keywords: Rust · Search-based testing · DynaMOSA

1 Introduction

In the programming language world, there are two major sides: low-level languages, which offer better performance at the expense of safety, and high-level languages, which provide safety for programmers through certain constructs such as garbage collection that lead to runtime overhead. The young programming language Rust tries to combine the best of both worlds: This statically typed language for system programming promises a similarly high performance as C++ while maintaining extended type and memory safety by default, avoiding problems such as dangling pointers, data races, integer overflows, buffer overflows, and iterator invalidation. This symbiosis makes the language particularly attractive to developers, which is demonstrated in a steady rise in popularity.

Even the Rust compiler cannot guarantee correctness, which means that one still has to check the software, e.g., with unit tests. The vast majority of existing search-based software testing (SBST) tools have been applied to managed languages since the ideas rely on the ability to use some sort of reflection and instrumentation. In contrast, Rust's source code is compiled directly into machine-executable code. It hardly provides any reflection capabilities, so both analysis and instrumentation of the System under Test (SUT) need to be done

M. Papadakis and S. R. Vergilio (Eds.): SSBSE 2022, LNCS 13711, pp. 3–18, 2022.
https://doi.org/10.1007/978-3-031-21251-2_1

during the compilation phase, i.e., statically. Another point in which Rust differs strongly not only from managed languages is its affine type system [1], which sets strict rules to how variables can be used. That is, they cannot be accessed and passed around freely. This fact changes the view on how to design a typical program in Rust. As a result, to the best of our knowledge there is no known use of SBST for Rust as of this writing.

In this paper, we aim to investigate this gap in the literature by addressing the problem of automatically generating test cases for Rust programs using a Genetic Algorithm (GA). The generated tests represent sequences of statements, i.e., they are built from a subset of the Rust language, and consider the peculiarities of the language's type and generic system. We implemented our approach as a wrapper around the original Rust compiler and hook into different compilation phases to execute our logic, such as extracting points of interest or instrumenting the SUT.

We evaluate our GA-based approach and compare it to the traditional baseline of random search to obtain certainty about the correctness of the implementation and any performance gain of our approach over the minimum. The evaluation is conducted using a case study built on our own library and a set of 6 real-world Rust libraries, or crates as they are called in Rust's jargon. We provide the implementation of the tool as well as the case study [15].

2 Background

2.1 The RUST Programming Language

Rust syntax is mostly in line with the C family of languages. Enums and structs are the custom data types available in Rust: Structs package related data together and are like an object's data attributes in object-oriented languages. Enums define a type by enumerating its possible variants, which are most often accessed via pattern matching, whereas struct fields can be accessed directly.

Associated Functions: Functions can be associated with types, e.g., with enums or structs. Rust separates the definition of behavior from the definition of data. Behavior for an enum or a struct is implemented in an `impl` block. Associated functions whose first parameter is named `self` are called methods and may be invoked using the method call parameter, for instance, `x.foo()`, as well as the usual function call annotation. `self` is an instance of the type `Self`, which, in the scope of a struct, enum, or trait, is an alias for the enclosing type. Through `self`, we can access the state and methods of the instance. In Listing 1.1, the struct `FixedSizeVector` has two associated functions: `new` and `size`.

Traits: A *trait* describes an abstract interface that types can implement, consisting of three types of associated items: functions, associated types, and constants. Traits are implemented through separate `impl` blocks. The struct in Listing 1.1 provides an implementation of the trait `HasSize` in lines 15–19.

Generics and Trait Objects: Rust supports generic types and allows for shared behavior via traits. Generics parametrize data structures and functions, such that different types can reuse the same code. This improves usability and helps find type errors statically. The language provides static and dynamic dispatch. The former is realized through monomorphization, i.e., for each type a generic implementation is used with, the compiler generates a concrete implementation of it and replaces the call sites with calls to the specialized functions.

Trait objects are usual instances of any type that implements the given trait, where the precise type can only be known at runtime. A function that takes trait objects is not specialized to each type that implements the trait: only one copy of the code is generated, resulting in less code bloat. However, this comes at the cost of requiring slower virtual function calls.

Listing 1.1. Example implementation of a generic vector struct with fixed size

```
1   trait HasSize {
2     fn size(&self) -> usize;
3   }
4
5   struct FixedSizeVector<T, const N: usize> {
6     elements: [T; N]
7   }
8
9   impl<T: Copy + Default, const N: usize> FixedSizeVector<T, N> {
10    fn new() -> Self {
11      Self { elements: [Default::default(); N] }
12    }
13  }
14
15  impl<T, const N: usize> HasSize for FixedSizeVector<T, N> {
16    fn size(&self) -> usize {
17      self.elements.len()
18    }
19  }
```

It is also possible to use trait bounds, i.e., constraints on generic type parameters. Bounding ensures that generic instances are allowed to access the methods of traits specified in the bounds. In Listing 1.1, the vector features a generic element type T which is constrained to implement Copy and Default traits.

Unlike object-oriented languages, there is no inheritance in Rust. Common behavior can be defined via traits, which can have super-traits. Besides structs, it is also possible to parametrize methods and functions using generics. Traits may also contain additional type parameters, which may be constrained by other traits. Usually, the more constraints, the more difficult it is to find correct types and automatically generate test cases that use those features and are compilable. Listing 1.1 demonstrates that there might be different constraints for the same type parameter (T) in different implementation contexts, and the program is compilable, as we do not need any in the trait implementation. They are still required to instantiate the struct, and it is not trivial to find the correct type to comply with the appropriate set of constraints when generating tests.

Ownership and Borrowing: In Rust, each value has an owner. There can only be one owner of a value at a time, and once the owner goes out of scope, the value is deallocated. For instance, the owner of a named value is the variable that is initialized with that value. Literal expressions, e.g., a character or an integer, are owned by the program itself and have a static lifetime. In cases where the value needs to outlive a given scope, it can be moved to a new owner in a different scope. This happens, for example, when a value is passed as a parameter to a function, or on assignment, with the caveat that values allocated on the stack are so cheaply copied that a move is never necessary.

Variable references can be immutable or mutable, meaning that the reference owner has write access. Creating a reference is also known as borrowing, a fundamental interaction aspect in the ownership model. The reference owner cannot modify the value by default when borrowing a value. It can only be borrowed mutably if it is not referenced somewhere else during the borrowing. The restrictive ownership model has particular implications for generating tests, i.e., we cannot use variables arbitrarily and need to observe their ownership state.

Lifetimes: A lifetime is an important aspect of borrowing and ensures that all borrows are valid. A variable's lifetime begins when it is created and ends when it is destroyed. When we borrow a variable with &, the lifetime of the borrow begins. Its end is determined by where the reference is still used.

2.2 Test Generation for Rust

Existing approaches for automatically testing Rust programs are mainly based on fuzzing tools: AFL++ is a reengineered fork of the popular coverage-guided fuzzer AFL [16], and *afl.rs* provides the ability to apply AFL++ to Rust. LLVM libFuzzer is another coverage-guided evolutionary fuzzing engine. Some tools build upon the libFuzzer and extend it with techniques like concolic testing [9,12]. Both LLVM libFuzzer and AFL++ require manually written fuzz targets, though, i.e., a chain of invocations and a recipe where to put the generated data. RULF is a fuzz target generator that, given the application programming interface (API) specification of a Rust library, can generate a set of fuzz targets and seamlessly integrate them with AFL++ for fuzzing [8]. An essential limitation of the tool is its inability to analyze and fuzz generic components. SyRust explicitly targets Rust's polymorphism and tries to generate compilable tests by applying a semantic-aware synthesis algorithm [14]. The tool handles the complicated trait system of the language by analyzing the compiler error messages and iteratively refining the extracted API information from the SUT, but for scalability reasons only targets few APIs in a crate at a time.

2.3 Search-Based Unit Test Generation

A state of the art approach to generate unit tests is by using the many-objective search algorithm DynaMOSA [11], which is an extension to the many-objective sorting algorithm (MOSA) [10]. Unlike a standard genetic algorithm, MOSA considers each coverage target as an independent objective. Its peculiarity is the preference sorting criterion to reward best test cases for each previously uncovered target. In addition, the algorithm uses an archive to store tests that cover new targets across iterations, rather than just returning best tests from the last iteration. DynaMOSA addresses the problem that objectives are often not independent of each other, e.g., the execution of one branch may depend on the execution of another branch. DynaMOSA dynamically selects targets based on the dependencies between the uncovered targets and the newly covered targets.

3   Search-Based Unit Test Generation for Rust

RUSTYUNIT is a tool that implements search-based test generation for Rust. It is based on established methods implemented in EVOSUITE [6], and uses the DynaMOSA algorithm to optimize tests for code coverage. The central differences of RUSTYUNIT over prior work lie in the encoding, which has to ensure that valid Rust code is produced, and the implementation of analysis, instrumentation, and test execution, which are essential for guiding the search algorithm.

3.1   Encoding

RUSTYUNIT models a chromosome as a test case, a sequence of statements or program calls that execute parts of the SUT to reach and cover a particular objective. We also need to take into account that Rust programs are not just procedures but have a certain class-like structure. Test cases only need to call functions with certain input data to achieve high coverage within a procedure-like environment. However, instances of structs can have states that direct accesses or method invocations can change. Similar to EVOSUITE's definition [5], each statement s_i in a test case is a value $v(s_i)$, which has a type $\tau(v(s_i)) \in \mathcal{T}$, where $\mathcal{T}$ is the finite set of types. There can be six different types of statements:

- **Primitive statements** represent numeric variables, e.g., `let v = 42`. The primitive variable defines the value and type of the statement.
- **Struct initializations** generate instances of a given struct, e.g., `let b = Book { name: "The Hobbit" }`. The object constructed in the statement defines the value and statement's type. A struct instantiation can have parameters whose values are assigned out of the set $\{v(s_k) \mid 0 \le k < i\}$.
- **Enum initializations** generate instances of a given enum, e.g., `let opt: Option<i32> = None;`. The enum instance defines the value and statement's type. An enum instantiation can have parameters whose values are assigned out of the set $\{v(s_k) \mid 0 \le k < i\}$.
- **Field statements** access member variables of objects, e.g., `let b = a.x`. The member variable defines the value and the field's statement type. The source of the member variable, i.e., a, must be part of the set $\{v(s_k) \mid 0 \le k < i\}$. Since unit tests are usually contained in the same module as the unit under test, tests can also legally access private fields.

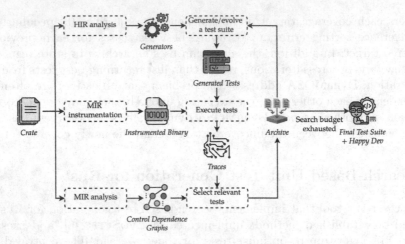

Fig. 1. The architecture of RUSTYUNIT

- **Associative function statements** invoke associative functions of datatypes, e.g., let b = a.len(). The owner of the function (if non-static) and all of the parameters must be values in $\{v(s_k) \mid 0 \le k < i\}$. The return value determines the statement's value and type. In the following, we refer to associative functions, too, when we talk about functions, unless otherwise stated.
- **Function statements** invoke loose functions, i.e., functions that are not associated with any datatype, for instance, let a = foo(). The parameters of the function must be values in $\{v(s_k) \mid 0 \le k < i\}$. The return value determines the statement's value and type.

3.2   Implementation

To generate tests for a crate, RUSTYUNIT has to complete several intermediate steps that Fig. 1 illustrates:

1. First and foremost, the tool requires information about which data types the *Crate* has and which functions the data types provide in order to be able to model meaningful tests in the first place. Therefore, it performs analysis at the High-level Intermediate Representation (HIR) level. HIR is a desugared and compiler-friendly representation of the abstract syntax tree that is generated after parsing, macro expansion, and name resolution. It is still close to what the user wrote syntactically, but it includes implicit information such as elided lifetimes and generated implementations. Also, some expression forms have been converted to simpler ones, e.g., for loops are converted to a more basic loop. The HIR analysis yields a collection of *Generators*. These provide an overview of which data types can be instantiated in a test case, and which methods can be invoked on those instances. RUSTYUNIT also derives the

ownership rules at this point, e.g., whether and how multiple statements may use a certain variable in a valid way, as described in Sect. 3.1.

2. To evaluate the *Generated Tests* in terms of their coverage, RUSTYUNIT instruments the Mid-level Intermediate Representation (MIR) and compiles the crate yielding an *Instrumented Binary*. MIR is a Control Flow Graph (CFG). It shows the basic blocks of a program and how control flow connects them. During instrumentation, the tool injects instructions into the MIR to trace the execution of individual basic blocks and branches. If a generated test executes a code location in the crate, the event is stored in the *Execution Traces*. If an executed basic block is an entry point of a branch, RUSTYUNIT computes how the values, which the conditional depends on, need to be changed to hit other branches in that context, i.e., branch distance (BD). The BD is 0 for all basic blocks that a test case executes.

3. The collected BDs in the execution traces are only one part. To calculate the overall fitness value with respect to each coverage target, RUSTYUNIT must additionally determine the approach level (AL) from the corresponding *Control Dependence Graphs* (CDGs), which it computes by analyzing the MIR of a SUT. This implies building a post-dominator tree from the CFG, which a MIR effectively is, and then computing the control dependencies. AL describes how far a test case was from a target in the corresponding CDG when the test case deviated from the course, i.e., the number of missed control dependencies between the target and the point where the test case took a wrong turn. With the CDGs and execution traces in place, RUSTYUNIT calculates the overall fitness value of a test t with respect to target m as follows:

$$F_m(t) = \text{Approach Level} + \alpha(\text{Branch Distance})$$

To ensure that the branch distance, which can become very large, does not dominate approach level, we use the normalization function α proposed by Arcuri [2]:

$$\alpha(x) = \frac{x}{x+1}$$

That is, the goal is to push the fitness value F of a test case with respect to a coverage target to zero to cover the target. In each iteration, RUSTYUNIT selects test cases that execute previously uncovered coverage targets and stores them in the *Archive*.

4. Now, RUSTYUNIT can either generate a new population and evolve it in the next iteration, or, when the search budget is exhausted, return the archive, i.e., the best tests found up to that point in the form of Rust source code.

RUSTYUNIT implements these steps using compiler hooks, which invoke our callbacks that perform analysis steps at an appropriate point of time. The tool also employs a constant pool analysis in which it extracts string and numerical constants from the source code, and several testability transformations based on prior work by Fraser and Arcuri [6]. That is, RUSTYUNIT exploits assertions that the Rust compiler automatically inserts in some cases in the MIR of a program, e.g., to check whether an array is accessed with an appropriate index or an integer addition does not overflow. Such an assertion is a branching point with one of the branches leading to a program crash. Thus, RUSTYUNIT tries to direct the search into covering the failure branches generated by the compiler.

Handling Generics and Traits: When tests are generated for generic elements, it is sometimes difficult to replace a generic type parameter with a matching concrete type because execution depends on the one concrete type [7]. The problem of generics becomes relevant whenever the test generation algorithm attempts to instantiate a new instance of a generic type, or to satisfy a parameter for a newly inserted method call. There are two scenarios of how RUSTYUNIT handles statements with generic types: If RUSTYUNIT generates a statement whose return value is to be used as a parameter for another statement, the tool replaces the generic type parameters of the return type by concrete ones, while any other generic types are chosen at random; for instance, to generate an argument of type Option<i32>, RUSTYUNIT could invoke foo from Listing 1.2 with type parameter A being i32. Since B is not constrained by the concrete return type and any trait bounds, the type is free to choose. Otherwise, all generic type parameters of the corresponding statement are selected randomly.

Listing 1.2. Generic types A and B are used as parameters and return value

```
1  impl<A, B> for FooBar<A, B> {
2    fn foo(&self, x: B, v: &Vec<A>) -> Option<A> { /* ... */ }
3  }
```

In general, RUSTYUNIT mainly uses primitive data types for a SUT to keep the generated tests simple as far as this satisfies the defined trait bounds.

Test Execution: With Cargo, Rust provides a build system and a testing framework out-of-the-box. In Java, generated tests can be executed directly using Reflection and bytecode instrumentation, and coverage information can be collected in the same runtime process. In Rust, we need to run the tests "traditionally", i.e., synthesize them into Rust source code, write them into the appropriate source file of the SUT, compile, and execute. Due to incremental compilation, the compiler generally only needs to recompile the changed test modules. Nevertheless, this introduces a non-negligible runtime overhead that RUSTYUNIT tries tominimize by compiling all tests in a population at once and concurrently executing them.

4   Evaluation

4.1   Experimental Setup

For evaluation we randomly chose 6 open-source crates from the Cargo's crate registry, resulting in a total of 2,965 functions and 12,842 MIR-level branches. The libraries were chosen with respect to their testability: For experiments, it is

Table 1. Number of lines of code, functions, and MIR-level branches in the case study subjects

Case study	Version	LOC	Functions	Branches
time	0.3.7	5123	1158	1147
gamie	0.7.0	328	116	594
lsd	0.21.0	3151	654	5609
humantime	2.1.0	414	87	437
quick-xml	0.23.0	3408	832	2025
tight	1.0.1	921	118	3030
Σ		13,345	2,965	12,842

necessary that the units are testable without complex interactions with external resources (e.g., databases, networks, and filesystem) and are not multi-threaded. We also ignored crates that used native features such as foreign function interfaces. Table 1 summarizes the properties of the case study subjects in terms of the number of functions, branches, and lines of code.

We limited the length of test cases to $L = 100$ because we experienced this to be a suitable length at which the test execution does not take too long, although the initial test cases are generated with only 30 statements each. The population size for the GA was chosen to be 50. Additionally, we evaluated two versions of the GA of RUSTYUNIT, seeded and non-seeded. The seeded version uses two optimizations. First, it samples available functions from the SUT in generated tests in a specific order determined by a ring buffer, so that all functions are guaranteed to be called in generated statements as long as enough tests are generated, rather than randomly sampling the functions. Second, it extracts constant literal values from the SUT's MIR and uses them with the probability of 0.4 whenever a primitive value is needed, instead of generating a random one.

For evaluation, we also implemented a random search algorithm in RUSTYUNIT, which generates random test cases in a manner similar to the initial population in the genetic algorithm of RUSTYUNIT, although it does not apply optimizations like recombination and mutation. It also exploits an archive and stores test cases that execute previously uncovered targets in a SUT. The random search approach in our evaluation uses the same probability parameters as those set for the genetic algorithms. We compare the algorithms using the MIR basic block coverage of test cases that remain after the algorithms have used up the budget of executed tests. Other objectives could also be used but are not implemented in RUSTYUNIT yet. The budget is set to $k = 5000$. To prevent long-running tests, we set a hard timeout of 3 s for the execution of a single test case using the *timeout* attribute from the *ntest*[1] crate. If a test execution exceeds the timeout, it gets aborted and its coverage is recorded only until that

---

[1] https://web.archive.org/web/20220522213803/https://crates.io/crates/ntest.

point. For each case study subject and each algorithm, we ran the experiments 30 times with different seeds for the random number generator to minimize the influence of randomness.

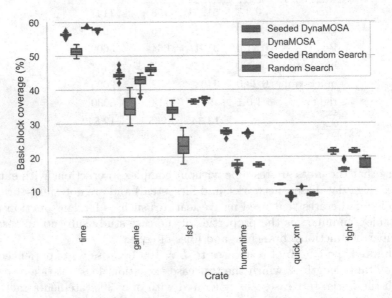

Fig. 2. Basic block coverage results per crate

4.2 Results

The boxplot in Fig. 2 compares the actual obtained basic block coverage values over 30 runs of RustyUnit's GA and random search on the 6 open-source crates. In total, the coverage improvement of RustyUnit using the seeded DynaMOSA ranged up to 5% than that of random search. Meanwhile, vanilla DynaMOSA performed worse on every crate in the case study. Calculated on all the crates we evaluated, seeded DynaMOSA obtained an average coverage of 32%, whereas random search and vanilla DynaMOSA obtained 31% and 23%, respectively. The overall coverage results are not particularly high mostly due to traits that we cannot handle or types that are too advanced for our primitive analysis. For instance, we do not call functions that derived traits provide, e.g., `Serialize` and `Deserialize` by the *serde* crate, which is a wide-spread (de-)serialization library found in almost any mature crate. Other than that, seeded DynaMOSA missed a few functions which random search did not miss; for example, the `new` functions of some structs, which, once called, get covered completely due to branchless structure. Similar limitations apply to the other crates. It seems that at this point, a higher number of hit functions still plays a greater role than local search of uncovered decision branches. This is also indicated by the fact that the seeded GA performs much better than its vanilla variant. Our seeding strategy incorporates sampling all possible methods from the SUT one-by-one and usage of the SUT's constant pool. However, the first three crates hardly contain any constants RUSTYUNIT can practically leverage.

The squeezed boxes in the Fig. 2 suggest that the better performing algorithms have reached the technical limit of our implementation in quite every run for each crate. However, random search has a slight lead for some crates, i.e., *time*, *gamie*, and *lsd*, while the results of seeded algorithms are roughly similar for the remaining ones, that is, *humantime*, *quick_xml*, and *tight*. For the latter ones, even vanilla DynaMOSA has caught up. The results seem to confirm the findings of Shamshiri et al. [13] who demonstrated that for branchless code or functions having predominately plateau branches, random search can yield at least as good coverage values as GAs, while GAs excel at gradient branches. Plateau branches are, for instance, comparisons of boolean values returned by a function call; we cannot compute a meaningful distance for those branches to guide genetic search, as opposed to gradient branches, e.g., comparisons of two integers. The average depth of the CDGs for *time* and *gamie* is close to 1, which is a sign that most of their functions are shallow, or branchless, i.e., most basic blocks are control dependent on the root of the respective CDG. The phenomenon especially involves generated functions, e.g., derived trait implementations. In turn, a shallow function code structure means that it is sufficient to call it once to reach all basic blocks, which is why random search achieves decent results on the evaluated crates. That also means that RUSTYUNIT cannot develop its full potential and employ guided search as it is mainly dependent on branch distances, which for plateau branches can only be 0 or 1. As a result, for some crates, random search continues to generate new test cases independently and hits more uncovered functions faster, while the genetic algorithm tries to surgically improve test cases that often cannot be improved in terms of fitness.

However, things look a bit different for *humantime*, *quick_xml*, and *tight*. *humantime* and *quick_xml* feature a greater control dependence depth, which is where both genetic algorithms start to shine at, as they now can additionally leverage approach level for the fitness calculation. The average depth value of *quick_xml* is relatively low, though. At this point, however, our seeding strategy helps the GA perform successfully. *quick_xml* is an XML parser library, whose API makes certain assumptions about the textual input it receives. For instance, consider the implementation block for the **new** function of the **BangType** enum in Listing 1.3, which, based on the input byte, decides which variant to return. RUSTYUNIT was able to extract the constant byte values used in the function and inserted one of them in the test 4410.

The byte 91 is the ASCII value for '['. That is, RUSTYUNIT successfully covered one of the branches. That one is quite simple, though. Listing 1.4 demonstrates another case of RUSTYUNIT being able to extract and use a constant value successfully. The function **local_name** returns its name after stripping the namespace, which is separated with a double colon usually. **memchr** is a function that returns an **Option** with the index of the first occurrence of a symbol in a

Listing 1.3. Enum `BangType` is part of the *quick_xml* crate

```
impl BangType {
  fn new(byte: Option<u8>) -> Result<Self> {
    Ok(match byte {
      Some(b'[') => Self::CData,
      Some(b'-') => Self::Comment,
      Some(b'D') | Some(b'd') => Self::DocType,
      Some(b) => return Err(Error::UnexpectedBang(b)),
      None => return Err(
        Error::UnexpectedEof("Bang".to_string())
      ),
    })
  }
}

#[test]
fn rusty_test_4410() {
  let mut u8_0: u8 = 91u8;
  let mut option_0: Option<u8> = Option::Some(u8_0);
  let result_0: Result<BangType> = BangType::new(option_0);
}
```

Table 2. For each crate, the table reports the average basic block coverage obtained by random search and DynaMOSA with seeding (and without)

Case study	RS	DynaMOSA	$\hat{A}_{12}$	p-value
time	0.58	0.56 (0.51)	0.11 (0.0)	<0.001 (<0.001)
gamie	0.46	0.44 (0.34)	0.10 (0.0)	<0.001 (<0.001)
lsd	0.37	0.35 (0.23)	0.22 (0.0)	<0.001 (<0.001)
humantime	0.18	0.23 (0.18)	1.0 (0.52)	<0.001 (<0.001)
quick-xml	0.09	0.12 (0.08)	1.0 (0.17)	<0.001 (<0.001)
tight	0.18	0.22 (0.17)	0.96 (0.12)	<0.001 (<0.001)
Average	0.31	0.32 (0.25)	0.52 (0.13)	

string. If the `name` does not have a namespace, `local_name` just returns the `name` as is, otherwise it strips the namespace by returning a slice starting at `i + 1`.

In test 3247, RUSTYUNIT invokes the function `local_name` and builds a dependency sequence, which initially uses a constant string "Attr::Empty" in Line 10. RUSTYUNIT again extracted the string value out of the constant pool of the SUT. Since the string contains a colon, the execution hits the *true* case when invoking `local_name` in Line 15. In summary, although the crate *quick_xml* does not feature a particularly high control dependence degree, RUSTYUNIT's seeded GA can still outperform random search using the seeding strategy.

Listing 1.4. Struct `BytesStart` is part of the *quick_xml* crate

```
impl<'a> BytesEnd<'a> {
  pub fn local_name(&self) -> &[u8] {
    let name = self.name();
    memchr::memchr(b':', name).map_or(name, |i| &name[i + 1..])
  }
}


#[test]
fn rusty_test_3247() {
    let mut str_0: &str = "Attr::Empty";
    let mut bcd_0: BytesCData = BytesCData::from_str(str_0);
    let mut cow_0: Cow<[u8]> = BytesCData::into_inner(bcd_0);
    let mut be_0: BytesEnd = BytesEnd {name: cow_0};
    let mut be_0_ref: &BytesEnd = &be_0;
    let mut u8_slice_0: &[u8] = BytesEnd::local_name(be_0_ref);
}
```

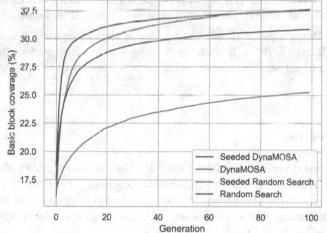

Fig. 3. Average basic block coverage development over generations

To better understand whether RUSTYUNIT's algorithm generally performs better, we provide statistical results in Table 2. The table presents the $\hat{A}_{12}$ effect size values with respect to the basic block coverage we obtained for the crates in the case study. We report the statistics of both, seeded and vanilla versions of the GA (in brackets) in comparison to random search. For instance, for *tight*, the $\hat{A}_{12}$ value of 0.96 means that the seeded DynaMOSA obtained a higher coverage in 96% of the cases. The table also provides results of the Mann-Whitney U test that we conducted per crate with the H0 hypothesis that each pair of the algorithms evaluated do not differ in terms of achieved coverage. We obtained p-values lower than the traditional $\alpha = 0.05$ for all crates, which means that the coverage differences over 30 executions are statistically significant. The seeded DynaMOSA could only achieve better effect sizes for 3 out of the 6 crates.

All algorithms only achieve moderately high coverage up to 58%. The main reason is that our analysis of the possible function invocations and types is still very limited. We cannot execute functions of many generic traits since those either require some advanced type and constraint analysis, or parameters that we cannot instantiate. For instance, in case of `Debug`, which is one of the most often implemented traits, its only method `fmt` requires an argument of type `std::fmt::Formatter` that RUSTYUNIT is not able to create using the current implementation state. Usually, the parameter is provided automatically by the compiler during macro expansion when one prints a value of a certain type that implements `Debug`, e.g., with `print!()`.

Figure 3 illustrates the development of the average basic block coverage over all crates over the available 100 generations. For random search, we split the generated test cases into chunks to match the progress of the two other algorithms. The line plot clearly indicates that the seeding strategy chosen has great impact on the performance of the GA. It also outperforms random search on average. In summary, we can answer the second research question as follows:

> **Summary:** Despite the shallow search space of the crates used, which inhibits the search, RUSTYUNIT still achieves a comparable coverage to random test generation, and for some crates, it achieves a significantly better coverage.

5   Conclusions

In this paper, we described our first foray into the challenging task of generating unit tests for Rust code. This popular new language offers many new fundamental and engineering challenges. As our evaluation suggests, our RUSTYUNIT prototype tool manages to address many of these challenges, but there are many remaining ones for future work. In particular:

- Traits: One of the most important aspects of Rust's type system and, at the same time, the biggest technical limitation of RUSTYUNIT are traits, which can become very complex and require advanced static analysis. To produce compilable test cases that at least can invoke all possible functions in a SUT and, moreover, achieve acceptable coverage results, one needs a sophisticated approach to model the underlying type system, analyze constraints, and map implementations to all appropriate datatypes. SyRust [14] presents a possible approach to repairing tests that do not compile due to type errors in the context of polymorphism.
- MIR: Rust compiles compound Boolean expressions into diamond-like subgraphs at the MIR level. Therefore, it is not trivial to determine what subexpression played a key role during a short-circuit evaluation and to trace the correct branch distance.

- Enums: Enumerations are first-class citizens in Rust. For instance, the two most prominent enums, `Option` and `Result`, can be found in any crate using the standard library. In contrast to other languages, enums are more powerful: Their variants can wrap other datatypes or be structs themselves. Datatype wrapping is especially a challenge when looking for suitable generators, if a generator returns a datatype wrapped (possibly multiple times) into an enum. Simply checking equality of types will fail in those cases.
- Tooling: Rust is a very young programming language, which implies that the variety of tools tailored for very specific tasks is not yet as rich as it is for other languages. For instance, there are no tools for program instrumentation such as Javassist [4] or ASM [3] for Java. Therefore, we needed to write our own compiler wrapper that parses crates' internals and injects atomic instructions for tracing. Given the size and complexity of the language, we had to limit it to a reasonable minimum. Thus, the prototype of RUSTYUNIT does not support many language features of Rust, like slices or lamdas.

To support further research on test generation for Rust, RUSTYUNIT is available as open source: https://github.com/toxycom/rusty-unit.

References

1. Anderson, B., et al.: Engineering the servo web browser engine using rust. In: Proceedings of the 38th International Conference on Software Engineering Companion, pp. 81–89. ACM (2016)
2. Arcuri, A.: It really does matter how you normalize the branch distance in search-based software testing. Softw. Tes. Verif. Reliab. **23**(2), 119–147 (2013)
3. Bruneton, E., Lenglet, R., Coupaye, T.: ASM: a code manipulation tool to implement adaptable systems. Adapt. Extensible Component Syst. **30**(19) (2002)
4. Chiba, S.: Load-time structural reflection in Java. In: Bertino, E. (ed.) ECOOP 2000. LNCS, vol. 1850, pp. 313–336. Springer, Heidelberg (2000). https://doi.org/10.1007/3-540-45102-1_16
5. Fraser, G., Arcuri, A.: Evolutionary generation of whole test suites. In: International Conference on Quality Software, pp. 31–40. IEEE Computer Society (2011)
6. Fraser, G., Arcuri, A.: 1600 faults in 100 projects: automatically finding faults while achieving high coverage with EvoSuite. Empir. Softw. Eng. **20**(3), 611–639 (2013). https://doi.org/10.1007/s10664-013-9288-2
7. Fraser, G., Arcuri, A.: Automated test generation for Java generics. In: Winkler, D., Biffl, S., Bergsmann, J. (eds.) SWQD 2014. LNBIP, vol. 166, pp. 185–198. Springer, Cham (2014). https://doi.org/10.1007/978-3-319-03602-1_12
8. Jiang, J., Xu, H., Zhou, Y.: RULF: rust library fuzzing via API dependency graph traversal. In: 2021 36th IEEE/ACM International Conference on Automated Software Engineering (ASE), pp. 581–592. IEEE Computer Society (2021)
9. Le, H.M.: KLUZZER: whitebox fuzzing on top of LLVM. In: Chen, Y.-F., Cheng, C.-H., Esparza, J. (eds.) ATVA 2019. LNCS, vol. 11781, pp. 246–252. Springer, Cham (2019). https://doi.org/10.1007/978-3-030-31784-3_14
10. Panichella, A., Kifetew, F.M., Tonella, P.: Reformulating branch coverage as a many-objective optimization problem (2015)

11. Panichella, A., Kifetew, F.M., Tonella, P.: Automated test case generation as a many-objective optimisation problem with dynamic selection of the targets. IEEE Trans. Softw. Eng. **44**(2), 122–158 (2018)
12. Rocha, H., Menezes, R., Cordciro, L.C., Barreto, R.: Map2Check: using symbolic execution and fuzzing. In: TACAS 2020. LNCS, vol. 12079, pp. 403–407. Springer, Cham (2020). https://doi.org/10.1007/978-3-030-45237-7_29
13. Shamshiri, S., Rojas, J.M., Fraser, G., McMinn, P.: Random or genetic algorithm search for object-oriented test suite generation? In: Proceedings of the 2015 Annual Conference on Genetic and Evolutionary Computation, pp. 1367–1374. ACM (2015)
14. Takashima, Y., Martins, R., Jia, L., Păsăreanu, C.S.: Syrust: automatic testing of rust libraries with semantic-aware program synthesis. In: Proceedings of the 42nd ACM SIGPLAN International Conference on Programming Language Design and Implementation, pp. 899–913. ACM (2021)
15. Tymofyeyev, V., Fraser, G.: Rustyunit search-based test generator for rust (2022). https://doi.org/10.5281/zenodo.7090044
16. Zalewski, M.: American fuzzy lop (2014)

An Empirical Comparison of EvoSuite and DSpot for Improving Developer-Written Test Suites with Respect to Mutation Score

Muhammad Firhard Roslan$^{(\boxtimes)}$, José Miguel Rojas, and Phil McMinn

University of Sheffield, Sheffield, UK
mfroslan2@sheffield.ac.uk

Abstract. Since software faults are usually unknown, researchers and developers rely on mutation analysis—i.e., seeding artificial defects, called mutants—to measure the quality of their test suites. One aim of *test amplification techniques* is to improve developer-written test cases so that they kill more mutants and potentially find more real faults. However, these tools tend to be limited in the types of changes and improvements they can make to tests, while also receiving little guidance to tests that kill new mutants. Alternatively, a tool like *EvoSuite* can generate tests with the benefit of detailed fitness information and have the benefit of more flexibility in terms of evolving a test's structure. However, the process is typically not based on developer-written tests, and consequently, the resulting test suites are less likely to be accepted by human developers. In this paper, we propose modifications to *EvoSuite*, in a technique we refer to as *EvoSuite$_{Amp}$*, which starts with developer-written tests as seeds, and then aims to evolve these tests in the direction of killing further mutants. We then empirically compare *EvoSuite$_{Amp}$* with a state-of-the-art test amplification tool, *DSpot*, on 42 versions of 29 different classes from the *Defects4J* benchmark, using the original developer-written test suites for each class as the starting point for test generation. In total, *EvoSuite$_{Amp}$* achieves a statistically better mutation score for 35 of these 42 versions when compared to *DSpot*.

Keywords: Search-based test case generation · Test amplification · Mutation analysis · Unit testing

1 Introduction

One of the challenges in software testing is deriving tests that are good at revealing faults [2]. But also, writing good tests manually is time-consuming, and some consider it to be a tedious task [30]. For this reason, there has been a lot of well-known work in automated test generation techniques, including in the search-based software engineering community [21].

A widely used automatic test generation tool for Java is *EvoSuite* [13], which generates JUnit tests. However, it has some limitations. Fundamentally, it cannot

M. Papadakis and S. R. Vergilio (Eds.): SSBSE 2022, LNCS 13711, pp. 19–34, 2022.
https://doi.org/10.1007/978-3-031-21251-2_2

solve the oracle problem [4]—human testers need to check that the assertions it generates are correct. Furthermore, the tests it generates do not typically involve human input, and require post-processing to make them more readable [8].

In contrast, *test amplification* explicitly aims to strengthen developer-written tests [9]. The aim is to generate a new version of the developer's test suite so that it covers more corner cases and is more effective at finding faults. Since the "amplified" test suite is based on the developers set of tests, it is likely more understandable and acceptable to them [6]. The current state-of-the-art test amplification tool, *DSpot* [10], utilizes developer-written tests to increase the number of mutants (artificially seeded defects [17]) that they kill. *DSpot* "amplifies" developer-written test cases by changing the values of literals in the tests, method calls, or by adding assertions. Test cases that kill more mutants and have fewer modifications are retained. However, test amplification tools themselves are subject to some limitations. Firstly, the types of changes they can make to tests are limited and not as flexible as *EvoSuite*'s evolution process. Furthermore, unlike search-based tools, they do not utilize fine-grained fitness information to guide them to new tests. Test cases generated by *DSpot* that do not kill new mutants, for example, will be discarded even if the test is actually "close" to killing a new mutant and could be usefully improved in future.

The aim of this paper is to evaluate a potential "best of both worlds" approach, in which we evaluate a version of *EvoSuite* that is capable of reading developer-written tests as a starting point for test case generation. Leveraging its ability to make more fundamental changes to the structure of a test case, it then evolves those tests with the benefit of fine-grained fitness information for killing new mutants. We then evaluate whether *EvoSuite*'s evolution and mutation analysis technique could have a better performance in terms of killing mutants when compared to *DSpot*'s amplification technique. The motivation behind this study is to understand how many more mutants *could* be killed by test amplification tools if the principles of test amplification were applied differently, in the flavor of a more flexible and more guided search-based style of approach.

We compare this modified *EvoSuite* version, which we refer to as $EvoSuite_{Amp}$, with *DSpot* using the developer-written tests in open source projects as the starting point for test suite generation—specifically, 42 different versions of 29 different Java classes in 7 different projects of *Defects4J* (v2.0.0) [19]. Our experiments reveal that $EvoSuite_{Amp}$ outperforms *DSpot* for 35 of the 42 Java class versions studied in terms of mutation score achieved. Over 30 repeated runs, $EvoSuite_{Amp}$ was further capable of killing more "unique" mutants that *DSpot* was not able to kill in any run for 36 of these 42 subjects. $EvoSuite_{Amp}$ and all the data collected is available in our replication package [1].

In summary, the contributions of this paper are as follows:

1. A new test improvement strategy that utilizes the flexibility of *EvoSuite*, $EvoSuite_{Amp}$, that evolves test cases and leverages fitness information for killing specific mutants (Sect. 3).

2. An empirical study with seven open-source projects comparing $EvoSuite_{Amp}$ with an existing state-of-the-art test amplification tool, *DSpot* (Sect. 4).
3. Results and analysis of the effectiveness of both tools in terms of mutation score and mutants uniquely killed by each tool (Sect. 5).

2 Background

Mutation Analysis. Mutation Analysis is a way to evaluate the quality of a test suite [11]. The idea is to make small artificial changes, known as mutants, that mimic the mistakes that programmers could make in a program. Mutation Analysis tools generate mutants by applying a set of rules, known as *mutation operators*, to the program. The program that contains the mutants is executed against the test suite, to assess the quality of the tests in it. If the result of running the mutated program is different from the original program, the mutant is considered *killed*, and if it is the same, the mutant is considered *alive* indicating that the test suite needs some change/improvement to kill it. The proportion of mutants that are killed as a percentage of all the mutants seeded is known as the test suite's *mutation score*. A test suite that achieves a higher mutation score is generally considered better at detecting faults than one with a lower score [15].

Test Amplification. Unit test suites are usually written by developers manually. This is a common practice as developers who wrote the program have domain knowledge about the program [2]. A study by Grano et al. [16] shows that tests that have been written by a developer tend to be more readable than those automatically generated by a tool. However, the biggest challenge is to create a good test suite that can detect faults [20]. Test amplification, a technique that improves a test suite by utilizing the existing developer-written tests could improve a variety of goals, such as improving code coverage and mutation score [9]. The main distinction between test amplification and general automated test generation tools is that test amplifiers use existing developer-written tests as a starting point, that they aim to improve/"amplify".

Two main parts of the process of test amplification are *input amplification* and *assertion amplification*. Input amplification involves forming new test cases by changing values, literals, objects, or method calls in some original, developer-written test case. Assertion amplification involves adding new assertion statements to the test that verify the expected output of the amplified inputs. After amplifying the inputs and assertions, a test amplification tool will derive several new test cases from the developer-written tests. A test selector then selects the test cases that kill new mutants with the fewest modifications from the original developer-written tests they were based on.

DSpot [10] is a well-known test amplification tool that amplifies developer-written tests. It takes, as input, the developer-written tests and the class that will be tested. The amplifiers used in input amplification of *DSpot* are the changing of literal values and method calls (by duplicating calls, removing them, or adding new invocations). After the tool amplifies the inputs, it further changes a test case by adding new assertions. Finally, to select which test cases are to be kept, *DSpot* measures the test cases based on the criteria that are used by the test selector it is configured with. The default test selector of *DSpot* uses the *PITest* mutation analysis tool [7] (a configuration of *DSpot* we refer to as $DSpot_{Mut}$), which keeps test cases that kill mutants not killed by the original test suite, and the number of changes from the original test case (with smaller changes preferred over bigger ones). Another test selector option available on *DSpot* uses the $JaCoCo^1$ coverage test selector (that we refer to as $DSpot_{Cov}$), which keeps test cases that increase code coverage and execute unique paths.

Search-Based Test Generation. *EvoSuite* is an automatic test generation for Java that uses genetic algorithms to generate a test suite [13] that has been evaluated on many open-source projects in terms of code coverage and detecting faults [31]. The default configuration of *EvoSuite* can produce a JUnit test suite that maximizes the code coverage for each class. However, it can also be configured to use a fitness function that aims to maximize the generated test suite's mutation score [14]. The fitness function that guides test generation towards strongly killing mutants is formulated using three different distance metrics. Firstly, it calculates the distance of the calling function on the test case if it does not contain the function of the mutated statement. Secondly, it calculates the distance to executing the mutant using the approach level and branch distance Finally, it calculates the mutation impact, where the mutants need to infect the state and could propagate to an observable state.

EvoSuite typically starts by generating a random initial population of tests that calls the class methods. However, this population can bee seeded using a technique called *carving* [28] that harvests sequences of statements from the test cases of an existing test suite. Assuming that developers have written some tests, *EvoSuite* can take those tests and execute them to collect all potential reusable objects. The objects will then be inserted as part of a newly created test case (initialization). However, there are two limitations of this technique. It needs the developer-written tests to be converted into a representation that could be used in the *EvoSuite* search algorithm, and all the assertions from the developer-written tests will be removed. This means that it does not preserve exactly the same format that is being written by a developer.

3   Modifications Made to *EvoSuite—EvoSuite$_{Amp}$*

EvoSuite was originally designed to generate a test suite from scratch. In this study, we need *EvoSuite* to read developer-written tests, remove mutants that are killed by developer-written tests, and not to add new random test cases during the search. With this in mind, we made four different modifications to *EvoSuite*, which we refer to as *EvoSuite$_{Amp}$*, and are as follows:

1. Removing Killed Mutants by the Developer-Written Tests. We set the fitness criteria of *EvoSuite$_{Amp}$* to both branch coverage and strong

---

[1] Available at: https://www.eclemma.org/jacoco/.

mutation testing. Before starting the evolution, we remove the goals that were met by the developer-written tests. This is to make sure that the search focuses on the goals that are not covered yet. As an example, the class under test will have mutant A, X, Y, and Z. If the developer-written test could kill mutant X, Y, and Z, the only criteria that it needs to meet is to kill mutant A only.

2. Seeding Developer-Written Tests into the Initial Population of the GA. The second modification we made is on the initial population of the test cases. The default behavior of *EvoSuite* is to randomly generate new test cases. Instead of randomly generating new test cases, we used the developer-written tests as the initial population of the search. This utilizes the developer's domain knowledge of the program. The initial population size on the *EvoSuite* is set to 50 individuals, but in our study, we changed the population size depending on the developer-written test suite size. This is all done by using the carving technique that has been implemented in *EvoSuite* [28], introduced in Sect. 2.

3. Tuning the Add New Random Test Case Rate to Zero. We tune the settings of the parameter values of the evolutionary algorithm responsible for generating the test suite. The default configuration of *EvoSuite* is to use crossover, mutation, and randomly add new test cases into the population. However, we change the rate of adding new random test cases to the population of test cases to zero. This change means that the developer-written tests are kept during evolution, without the addition of completely new, randomly generated tests. This is crucial for maintaining similarity of the generated tests to the original test suite, and keeping the test suite free of tests or part of tests that are completely new or alien to the original developer. We still allow modifications to inputs featuring in the tests, however, so that there is scope for improving the original tests to kill more mutants, and for tests to be recombined by the crossover operator. After a few generations, the fitness of all individual chromosomes improves, where it will stop if it meets all the criteria or if the search budget is exhausted. A study by Aniche et al. shows that developers tend to copy and paste from previous test methods and modify their name, inputs, and assertions [2]. This effect is simulated, in part, by crossover, with mutation focussed on modifying the developer-written test inputs only.

4. Turning Off Test Suite Minimization. We turned off the *EvoSuite* test suite post-process minimization feature in order to maintain the developer-written tests, else they may be discarded following test suite evolution.

4   Empirical Study

This section details the experiment design of the empirical study we conducted to assess $EvoSuite_{Amp}$, $DSpot_{Mut}$, and $DSpot_{Cov}$ with respect to killing mutants. We also include $DSpot_{Cov}$ into the experiment because the $EvoSuite_{Amp}$ fitness criteria includes branch coverage. In the following, we refer to $EvoSuite_{Amp}$ and

Table 1. Subject programs used in this study

Subject	Acronym	Lines of Code			Avg. # of Mutants	# of Unique Classes Evaluated	# of Versions Evaluated
		Min	Max	Avg.			
Commons-**Cli**	Cli	56	200	104	261	2	3
Commons-**Codec**	Cdc	162	355	242	253	3	4
Commons-**Compress**	Crs	92	370	205	182	5	5
Commons-**Csv**	Csv	105	1152	675	117	3	9
Jsoup	Jsp	85	280	193	48	5	7
Commons-**Lang**	Lng	52	1366	907	568	3	5
Commons-**Math**	Mth	148	1091	469	662	8	9
Total						29	42

DSpot as distinct "tools", while we breakdown the analysis of *DSpot* in terms of the two configurations $DSpot_{Mut}$ and $DSpot_{Cov}$ (Sect. 2 for more information). We designed our empirical study to answer the following four research questions:

RQ1: Which tool ($EvoSuite_{Amp}$ or *DSpot*) kills the most mutants?
RQ2: Which tool kills the most "unique" mutants (mutants not killed by the alternative tool)?
RQ3: Which tool kills the most mutants with the smallest test suites?
RQ4: Which tool provides the most consistent results when re-run multiple times?

Subjects. We performed our experiment on the widely used benchmark *Defects4J* (v2.0.0) [19], which contains 835 reproducible real faults on 17 open-source projects. Although we are not specifically interested in the individual bugs provided by this benchmark, it provides us with an ideal set of subject classes and utilities with which we can evaluate the performance of both the $EvoSuite_{Amp}$ and *DSpot* tools. This includes an interface for test generation, which among other things help with removing flaky tests—tests that pass and fail without any changes to code [26]. It also incorporates the *Major* [18] mutation analysis tool, which we use as independent arbiter of the mutants killed by the test suites generated by both $EvoSuite_{Amp}$ and *DSpot* tools (since *DSpot* relies on *PITest* [7], while *EvoSuite* uses its own in-built mutation analysis).

We selected subject classes from *Defects4J* with which to perform our experiment based on the following rules:

1. The project includes developer-written tests;
2. $DSpot_{Mut}$, $DSpot_{Cov}$, and $EvoSuite_{Amp}$ were capable of using the provided original developer-written tests,
3. *Major* [18], *PITest* [7], and *EvoSuite* could generate mutants for the project.

After running every faulty version of each project in the *Defects4J* dataset, 42 faulty versions of 29 unique classes in 7 libraries met the requirements above. Table 1 shows the details of these subjects. We found a large number of *Defects4J*'s classes/versions to be unusable for our study due to an issue with *DSpot*'s interface with its mutation analysis tool *PITest* needed for the study, and problems compiling the class under test. We have contacted the owner of the *DSpot* project, and it could not be resolved to date. Despite this, our final subject set comprises a wide and diverse set of classes over a number of projects that are suitable for our study.

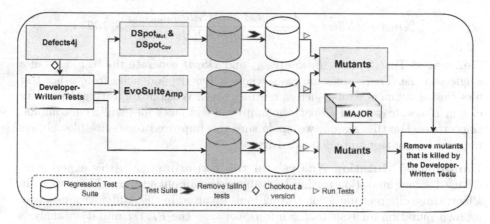

Fig. 1. Overview of the experimental setup. We amplified the test suite using *EvoSuite*$_{Amp}$, *DSpot*$_{Mut}$, and *DSpot*$_{Cov}$.

4.1   Experimental Procedure

Figure 1 shows the overview of our experiment. The tools are fed with developer-written tests that were gathered from the test files in every project version (with a particular fault) from *Defects4J*. For each version, as shown in Table 2, we improved each class of the study's original developer-written test suite (as provided by *Defects4J*) using *EvoSuite*$_{Amp}$ (using *EvoSuite* v1.2.0), and *DSpot*$_{Mut}$ and *DSpot*$_{Cov}$ (using v3.2.0 of *DSpot*). We ran all experiments on the same workstation, with 32 GB RAM and Intel i5 CPU @ 3.10 GHz, running Ubuntu 20.04.4 LTS. For both tools, we set the search budget time limit to 120 s, a commonly used value for test suite generation, and one that is applied in the search-based testing tool competition [25].

To take into account the non-deterministic nature of the tools, we repeat test suite generation 30 times for each tool/configuration studied. While we did not perform any internal modifications to *DSpot*—the build was downloaded from their repository[2] and configured to form *DSpot*$_{Mut}$ and *DSpot*$_{Cov}$. We made the modifications to *EvoSuite* to form *EvoSuite*$_{Amp}$ detailed in Sect. 3.

---

[2] Available at: https://github.com/STAMP-project/dspot.

To make sure that there will not be any failing (*flaky*) tests generated by either tool, we used the *fix_test_suite* feature of *Defects4J* that removes failing tests from the test suite until all of them pass. Without removing the failing tests, flaky tests could interfere with the mutation score result. For all the developer-written and generated regression test suites, we used the *Major* mutation testing tool [18] to compute the mutation score. *Major* includes a summary of which mutants are killed by each test suite. The summary helps in finding the additional number of mutants that the generated test suites kill. We calculate the relative increase of mutation score for each automatically improved test suite, over the original developer-written version as:

$$\%IncreaseKilled = \frac{AverageMutantsKilled_{Amplified}}{TotalNumberOfMutants} \times 100$$

Generated Test Suites. *EvoSuite*$_{Amp}$ and *DSpot* generate the test cases in a single test file. There are some cases where it has dependencies from other test files that developers wrote, such as a utility class. Without importing dependencies in *EvoSuite*$_{Amp}$ and *DSpot*, the improved test suite files will have compilation errors. For this reason, we made sure the improved test suite files always imported these test suite dependencies.

Handling of Mutation Analysis in the Experiment. In this experiment, we used strong mutation testing to evaluate the amplified tests. There were, in effect, three different mutation testing tools involved in the study. *EvoSuite* uses its own mutation analysis tool, while *DSpot* uses the *PITest* mutation analysis tool as part of its test amplification process. Since both *EvoSuite* and *DSpot* use different mutation analysis tools, it is not fair to compare the number of mutants it kills with different tools, which could produce different results for the same test suite. To avoid any bias in our study, we used a third mutation analysis tool, in the form of *Major* [18] to perform mutation analysis after both *EvoSuite* and *DSpot* generate the improved test suite. Since *Major* is *Defects4J*'s default mutation analysis tool, it was straightforward for us to apply this analysis.

Statistical Analysis. Since we are assessing algorithms that are making random choices, we analyzed the data that we collected using well-established statistical analysis recommendations [3]. We repeated each experiment 30 times. We then used the Mann-Whitney U-test to check for the significant differences regarding the number of mutants killed, comparing *EvoSuite*$_{Amp}$ with *DSpot*$_{Mut}$ improved test suites, and then *EvoSuite*$_{Amp}$ with *DSpot*$_{Cov}$ test suites, for each version of each subject class. We used the 99% confidence interval, which means that if the *p*-value is less than 0.01, our result is statistically significant. We further calculate effect sizes, using Vargha-Delaney's ($\hat{A}$) test. Again, we compared *EvoSuite*$_{Amp}$ with *DSpot*$_{Mut}$, and then *EvoSuite*$_{Amp}$ with *DSpot*$_{Cov}$. An $\hat{A}$ value that is over 0.5 indicates that *EvoSuite*$_{Amp}$ outperforms *DSpot*. Another statistical analysis that we performed was finding the correlation between the size of the test suite, and the mutation score. We used Spearman's rank correlation coefficient to find the relationship between the two variables. We used 99% confidence interval to indicate if the result is statistically significant.

4.2   Threats to Validity

Naturally, there are threats to validity associated with our study. The first is associated with subject selection. We chose to use versions of classes that are part of the *Defects4J* benchmark, yet not all of the classes it provides could be used in our study, due to problems in getting *DSpot* to work. However, we were able to use 42 versions of 29 unique classes in 7 projects, which still provides a suitable number and diversity of subjects with which to carry out our experiments and draw conclusions from the results. Another threat is related to how mutation score is calculated, since *EvoSuite* and *DSpot* use different mechanisms. *EvoSuite* provides its own implementation of a mutation analysis pipeline, while *DSpot* uses *PITest*. To control this threat, we used a third tool, *Major*, to provide an unbiased assessment across the results of the two tools. To control the threats related to the non-deterministic behavior of both tools, we repeated our experiments 30 times. To mitigate the threats associated with our statistical analysis, and assumptions about the normality of the statistical distributions of our results, we used non-parametric statistical tests. Finally, after generating the test cases using both $EvoSuite_{Amp}$ and *DSpot*, there are some cases where it needs other test files to run, due to dependencies. This could have an impact when calculating the mutation score. To mitigate this problem, we ensured all improved test suites retained access to any dependent libraries and code.

5   Results

Answer to RQ1: Mutation Score. Table 2, part B, shows the mean of the mutants killed by $EvoSuite_{Amp}$, $DSpot_{Mut}$, and $DSpot_{Cov}$. The table further shows that $EvoSuite_{Amp}$ is more effective at killing mutants for 35 out of the 42 versions (83.3%) than $DSpot_{Mut}$. It is also better at killing mutants for 27 out of the 42 (64.3%) versions compared to $DSpot_{Cov}$. $EvoSuite_{Amp}$ is most effective at killing mutants with classes from the *Math* project. All the class versions that $EvoSuite_{Amp}$ achieves a better mutation score have a p-value less than 0.01. Where $DSpot_{Cov}$ and $DSpot_{Mut}$ achieve a better mutation score than $EvoSuite_{Amp}$, the p-value is less than 0.01. When using the $\hat{A}$ statistic to measure effect size, we found that $EvoSuite_{Amp}$ has a score that favours it over $DSpot_{Mut}$ in 35 out of the 42 projects and $DSpot_{Cov}$ in 25 out of 42 versions (59.5%), each time with an $\hat{A}$ value greater than 0.8 (i.e., a large effect size).

Conclusion for RQ1. $EvoSuite_{Amp}$ performs better than $DSpot_{Mut}$ and $DSpot_{Cov}$ in terms of killing mutants.

Answer to RQ2: Unique Mutants. We also evaluated the cumulative number of uniquely killed mutants after executing each of the 30 test suites on every

Table 2. The result of test amplification on 42 versions after 30 runs for $EvoSuite_{Amp}$ (**Evo**), $DSpot_{Mut}$ (**DS**), and $DSpot_{Cov}$ (**DJ**).

(A) Fault Version	(B) # of Killed Mutants						(C) Standard Deviation			(D) # of Unique Mutants Killed			(E) Original TS Mutation Score %	(F) Increase Killed %			(G) # of KLOC		
	Mean			Median										Mean					
	Evo	DS	DJ	Evo	DS	DJ	Evo	DS	DJ	Evo	DS	DJ		Evo	DS	DJ	Evo	DS	DJ
Cdc-11	†18.2	16.5	20.0	†18.0	16.0	20.0	°1.2	1.2	0.0	20	20	20	63.9	†21.9	19.9	24.1	*0.2	0.1	0.3
Cdc-16	†°90.5	2.0	7.0	†°90.5	2.0	7.0	†°23.3	1.0	0.0	†°139.0	3	7	50.6	†°9.9	0.2	0.8	**0.7	<0.1	0.1
Cdc-17	†°7.3	1.0	2.0	†°7.5	1.0	2.0	°1.4	0.0	0.0	†°9.0	1	2	43.5	†°31.6	4.3	8.7	**0.3	0.2	0.3
Cdc-18	†°6.9	1.5	2.0	†°7.0	2.0	2.0	°1.5	0.5	0.0	†°9.0	2	2	43.5	†°30.0	6.7	8.7	**0.3	0.2	0.3
Cli-37	†°13.7	1.0	1.0	†°13.0	1.0	1.0	†°4.3	0.0	0.0	†°23.0	1	1	76.5	†°3.7	0.3	0.3	**1.4	<0.1	<0.1
Cli-38	†°10.8	2.0	2.0	†°11.0	2.0	2.0	†°2.4	0.0	0.0	†°15.0	2	2	76.1	†°2.9	0.5	0.5	**1.5	<0.1	<0.1
Cli-39	1.0	2.0	2.0	1.0	2.0	2.0	0.0	0.0	0.0	1	2	2	14.3	7.1	14.3	14.3	**0.2	<0.1	0.2
Crs-34	†°39.0	35.0	35.0	†°40.0	35.0	35.0	°3.0	0.0	0.0	†°44.0	35	35	48.2	†°34.8	31.2	31.2	**0.4	0.2	0.2
Crs-39	†°57.5	36.0	36.0	†°58.5	36.0	36.0	†°4.0	0.0	0.0	†°62.0	36	36	32.1	†°51.3	32.1	32.1	**0.8	<0.1	<0.1
Crs-40	†9.0	4.4	17.0	†9.0	4.0	17.0	°2.1	3.1	0.0	†15.0	12	17	37.2	†0.9	0.5	1.8	**0.2	<0.1	<0.1
Crs-44	12.1	15.3	17.0	12.5	14.0	17.0	°3.1	1.5	0.0	†18.0	17	17	0.0	52.6	66.5	73.9	**0.2	<0.1	<0.1
Crs-45	†°108.4	56.3	63.0	†°110.0	57.0	63.0	†°14.6	1.3	0.0	†°132.0	57	63	54.2	†°18.7	9.7	10.9	**0.8	0.2	0.2
Csv-01	†°6.7	2.1	3.0	†°6.5	3.0	3.0	†°2.9	1.1	0.0	†°16.0	3	3	41.7	†°8.0	2.5	3.6	**0.3	<0.1	0.5
Csv-02	†°9.6	2.0	7.0	†°12.0	2.0	7.0	†°3.3	0.0	0.0	†°12.0	2	7	36.8	†°50.5	10.5	36.8	**0.3	0.1	0.1
Csv-04	†16.8	14.8	27.0	†17.0	15.0	27.0	†°1.4	1.0	0.0	†20.0	18	27	40.0	†24.0	21.2	38.6	**0.3	0.3	0.9
Csv-06	†°12.2	8.4	9.0	†°12.0	8.0	9.0	†°0.6	0.5	0.0	†°13.0	9	9	35.0	†°61.2	41.8	45.0	**0.4	0.2	0.2
Csv-07	†14.7	12.9	23.0	†14.0	12.0	23.0	†°2.3	1.5	0.0	†19.0	16	23	47.1	†21.0	18.4	32.9	**0.3	0.2	1.0
Csv-10	16.2	56.0	108.0	14.5	54.5	108.0	°6.3	10.3	0.2	33	75	109	28.2	5.7	19.7	38.0	**0.6	0.2	0.5
Csv-11	†18.1	13.4	31.0	†18.0	13.0	31.0	°2.0	2.1	0.0	†23.0	18	31	42.0	†22.3	16.5	38.3	**0.3	0.2	1.0
Csv-12	†31.7	0.0	108.0	†33.0	0.0	108.0	†°3.4	0.0	0.0	†36.0	0	108	50.3	†10.1	0.0	34.6	**2.1	0.1	1.0
Csv-16	†22.4	12.2	46.0	†22.5	8.0	46.0	°4.3	7.4	0.0	†31.0	26	46	36.8	†19.6	10.7	40.4	**0.8	0.3	1.3
Jsp-58	9.7	20.1	29.0	8.0	19.0	29.0	†°4.4	2.2	0.0	23	25	29	22.5	13.7	28.4	40.8	**0.1	<0.1	0.2
Jsp-69	†14.3	2.0	24.0	†15.0	2.0	24.0	†°2.8	0.0	0.0	†18.0	2	24	2.6	†37.6	5.3	63.2	**0.2	0.1	0.4
Jsp-79	†°2.3	0.0	0.0	†°2.0	0.0	0.0	†°0.5	0.0	0.0	†°4.0	0	0	53.8	†°9.0	0.0	0.0	**0.2	0.2	0.3
Jsp-80	36.6	46.0	49.0	35.0	46.0	49.0	†°4.4	2.2	0.0	45	49	49	11.1	45.1	56.8	60.5	**0.3	<0.1	0.2
Jsp-84	16.0	26.0	27.0	16.0	26.0	27.0	°2.2	0.0	0.0	20	26	27	0.0	38.2	61.9	64.3	**0.2	0.1	0.1
Jsp-86	†°6.9	1.5	0.0	†°7.0	1.5	0.0	†°2.1	1.5	0.0	†°12.0	3	0	51.4	†°19.6	4.3	0.0	**0.2	<0.1	0.2
Jsp-93	†15.7	4.0	18.0	†16.0	4.0	18.0	†°2.6	0.0	0.0	†°19.0	4	18	2.5	†39.2	10.0	45.0	**0.3	0.2	0.4
Lng-03	†517.8	484.2	545.0	†517.5	485.0	545.0	†°12.2	8.9	0.0	†543.0	499	545	0.4	†58.2	54.5	61.3	**2.2	1.2	1.6
Lng-04	°0.8	1.0	0.0	°1.0	1.0	0.0	†°0.5	0.0	0.0	°2.0	1	0	82.9	°2.0	2.4	0.0	**0.3	<0.1	<0.1
Lng-05	†°104.0	5.0	8.0	†°104.0	5.0	8.0	†°3.1	0.0	0.0	†°112.0	5	8	0.0	†°73.8	3.5	5.7	**0.4	0.2	0.2
Lng-07	†°530.8	406.0	492.0	†°530.5	407.5	492.0	°11.0	13.3	0.0	†°554.0	449	492	0.4	†°59.3	45.4	55.0	**2.4	1.0	1.5
Lng-16	†520.7	416.2	490.0	†520.0	415.0	490.0	°10.9	12.8	0.0	†°545.0	445	490	0.5	†°59.6	47.7	56.1	**2.3	1.1	1.5
Mth-09	†°26.2	20.0	20.0	†°26.0	20.0	20.0	†°3.4	0.0	0.0	†°32.0	20	20	51.6	†°28.8	22.0	22.0	**0.4	0.9	1.7
Mth-25	†°112.9	41.9	82.0	†74.5	32.0	82.0	†°72.3	13.2	0.0	†°233.0	59	82	0.0	†°32.2	12.0	23.4	**0.3	<0.1	0.1
Mth-26	†°157.0	51.4	65.0	†°157.0	51.0	65.0	†°4.2	0.7	0.0	†°168.0	53	65	45.6	†°33.3	10.9	13.8	*1.0	0.8	1.2
Mth-27	†°152.1	51.2	65.0	†°152.0	51.0	65.0	†°3.4	0.6	0.2	†°157.0	53	65	46.0	†°32.6	11.0	13.9	*1.1	0.8	1.1
Mth-36	†°85.6	54.0	71.0	†°86.0	54.0	71.0	†°10.7	0.0	0.0	†°101.0	54	71	48.4	†°23.3	14.7	19.3	1.5	2.2	2.8
Mth-52	†°1509.6	181.0	187.0	†°1497.0	181.0	187.0	†°244.0	0.0	0.0	†°1869.0	181	187	6.0	†°55.1	6.6	6.8	**1.1	0.2	0.5
Mth-53	†244.1	88.3	307.0	†255.5	82.5	307.0	°60.0	24.2	0.0	†°311.0	142	307	26.5	†46.5	16.8	58.5	1.4	3.1	13.1
Mth-55	†°536.2	266.0	266.0	†°542.0	266.0	266.0	†°24.3	0.0	0.0	†°567.0	266	266	19.0	†°68.5	34.0	34.0	**1.5	0.8	1.0
Mth-56	†°89.8	45.0	47.0	†°90.0	45.0	47.0	†°9.5	0.0	0.0	†°111.0	45	47	0.0	†°57.2	28.7	29.9	**0.5	<0.1	<0.1

† $EvoSuite_{Amp}$ performs significantly better than $DSpot_{Mut}$ (p-value < 0.01)
o $EvoSuite_{Amp}$ performs significantly better than $DSpot_{Cov}$ (p-value < 0.01)
* $EvoSuite_{Amp}$ generates more KLOC than $DSpot_{Mut}$
• $EvoSuite_{Amp}$ generates more KLOC than $DSpot_{Cov}$

tool. This means that mutants that are still alive after 30 runs are considered as either stubborn mutants or equivalent mutants. We found that $EvoSuite_{Amp}$ killed more unique mutants in 36 out of the 42 versions (85.7%) when compared to $DSpot_{Mut}$, and 27 out of the 42 versions (64.3%) when compared to $DSpot_{Cov}$. This and more detailed information regarding the performance of each tool on each class version can be seen in part D of Table 2.

Conclusion for RQ2. $EvoSuite_{Amp}$ kills more unique mutants after 30 runs when compared to $DSpot_{Mut}$ and $DSpot_{Cov}$.

Table 3. Spearman correlation value (ρ) between test suite size (LOC) and mutation score.

Tool	p-value	Correlation (ρ)
$EvoSuite_{Amp}$	<0.01	0.698
$DSpot_{Mut}$	<0.01	0.588
$DSpot_{Cov}$	<0.01	0.608

Answer to RQ3: Size of Test Suite. Even though $EvoSuite_{Amp}$ can kill more mutants, it generates bigger test suites in general. When comparing $DSpot_{Mut}$ to $EvoSuite_{Amp}$, 39 out of the 42 class versions studied involved an improved test suite that is smaller number of lines of code (KLOC) when $DSpot_{Mut}$ was used, and when comparing $DSpot_{Cov}$ to $EvoSuite_{Amp}$, 26 out of the 42 class versions had smaller test suites with $DSpot_{Cov}$. Furthermore, when comparing $DSpot_{Mut}$ to $EvoSuite_{Amp}$, the improved test suites for 27 out of 42 class versions (64.3%) had a better ratio of killing mutants per line of code with $DSpot_{Mut}$, and similarly 26 out of 42 versions (61.9%) were better with $DSpot_{Cov}$ than $EvoSuite_{Amp}$. In all seven versions in which $DSpot_{Mut}$ has a better mutation score, it improves test suites with a smaller KLOC compared to $EvoSuite_{Amp}$. As an example, Cli-39 as shown in Table 2 part G, $EvoSuite_{Amp}$ generates 0.2 KLOC to kill one mutant, while $DSpot_{Mut}$ generates 0.1 KLOC to kill two mutants. When comparing $EvoSuite_{Amp}$ to $DSpot_{Cov}$, where $DSpot_{Cov}$ has a better mutation score, 8 out of 15 class versions (53.3%) have a lower number of LOC. As an example, for Cdc-11, $EvoSuite_{Amp}$ generates 0.2 KLOC while killing around 18 mutants and $DSpot_{Cov}$ generates 0.3 KLOC, while killing 20 mutants. On the contrary, Jsp-84, $EvoSuite_{Amp}$ generates 0.2 KLOC while killing around six mutants, and $DSpot_{Cov}$ generates 0.1 KLOC, while killing 27 mutants.

In order to verify whether there is a correlation between the generated test suite KLOC size and the increase of mutation score, we used the Spearman rank correlation measure. Table 3 presents the correlation coefficients of each tool. There is a strong correlation (ρ) between the $EvoSuite_{Amp}$ size of the test, and the increase in mutation score. In both $DSpot_{Mut}$ and $DSpot_{Cov}$, there is a moderate (ρ >0.4) correlation between the size and increase of the mutation score, and high correlation ($\rho > 0.7$) for $EvoSuite_{Amp}$. All the tools' p-values are less than 0.01, which shows that there is statistical significance.

> **Conclusion for RQ3.** $EvoSuite_{Amp}$ generates a larger final test suite when compared to $DSpot_{Mut}$ and $DSpot_{Cov}$.

Answer to RQ4: Consistency. In order to investigate the non-determinism rate on each tool, we calculated the mean, median, and standard deviation (σ) of the mutation score for all 42 subject class versions over each of the respective 30 re-runs. Table 2 (parts B and C) shows the result of the calculations. The mutation score $EvoSuite_{Amp}$ produces has a greater standard deviation when compared to $DSpot_{Mut}$ and $DSpot_{Cov}$. There were only 7 out of the 42 versions (16.6%) for which the $DSpot_{Mut}$ produced a higher standard deviation, while there was zero for $DSpot_{Cov}$.

> **Conclusion for RQ4.** $EvoSuite_{Amp}$ tends to show more varied behavior when compared to $DSpot_{Mut}$ and $DSpot_{Cov}$.

5.1   Discussion

We now discuss some of the ramifications of our results, along with further observations made during the course of the experiments.

Mutation Score. The $EvoSuite_{Amp}$ tool, in general, kills more mutants than $DSpot$, which shows that using the distance to mutation fitness function that is provided in $EvoSuite$ can kill mutants that $DSpot$ finds hard to kill. In the case of amplifying developer-written tests using $DSpot_{Cov}$, it is not surprising that an increase in code coverage also helped to increase the mutation score, as mutants that are not reached by developer-written tests could not be detected. Overall, the results show that $EvoSuite$'s evolution and mutation analysis technique is much more suited to improving test suites to kill mutants than $DSpot$.

Unique Mutants. Furthermore, $EvoSuite_{Amp}$ finds and kills more unique mutants after 30 runs when compared to $DSpot_{Mut}$ and $DSpot_{Cov}$. This shows that $EvoSuite$ explores more parts of the program than $DSpot$ within the 30 runs and that it could find more unique mutants, further adding to our finding that it is better at improving test suites to kill mutants than $DSpot$.

Test Suite Size. In answering RQ3, we found that $EvoSuite_{Amp}$ usually creates a bigger test suite when compared to the two configurations of $DSpot$, and that there is a high correlation between killing mutants and a big test suite. However, by looking at the mutants killed per number of lines of code, the value is not significantly bigger. We set $EvoSuite_{Amp}$ to not run the minimization technique that the default $EvoSuite$ does (see Sect. 3), to avoid original developer-written tests being discarded—however, enabling this technique could reduce the lines of code while maintaining the mutation score. We leave this experiment as an item for future work.

Consistency of Results. Finally, RQ4 shows that both $DSpot_{Mut}$ and $DSpot_{Cov}$ give more consistent results over the 30 runs with each subject class version. This potentially means, however, that $EvoSuite_{Amp}$ has a higher chance of exploring more edge cases due the higher degree of stochasticity that it evolves the developer-written tests, and thereby could find more unique mutants, as shown by the answer to RQ2.

Readability of Final Tests. Anecdotally, we noted that the tests produced by $EvoSuite_{Amp}$ were less readable than $DSpot$'s. Some of this was due to the inevitable disruption caused by the evolutionary operators (although we deliberately turned some of these off for this reason—see Sect. 4.1). In particular, the carving procedure adapts developer-written tests to EvoSuite's internal test case representation, which causes them to lose some of their original qualities. This is something that needs to be investigated in future work.

6 Related Work

There have been many works that have sought to generate tests based on existing tests, for example to speed up the process of test generation [32], or as seeds as the initial population of a search-based technique [12,28].

Test amplification is a research area that comprises techniques designed to *improve* a developer-written set of test cases in some aspect. One of these aspects is the test suite's coverage and mutation score [9]. There have also been techniques that attempt to improve new tests generated by the amplification process, for example with respect to their readability [22] and potential redundancy [24]. Popular test amplification tools include *DSpot* for Java [10], studied in this paper, and *AmPyfier* for Python [29]. *Test Cube* is a developer-centric test amplification tool for Java [6] that operates as a plugin for the IntelliJ integrated development environment, and builds on the techniques of *DSpot*.

However, none of these works directly compare test amplification tools with techniques capable of fine-grained fitness information to guide the test case search towards strongly killing mutants—functionality that is available in *EvoSuite*.

Elsewhere, Olsthoorn et al. [23] applied model seeding that could contribute improving mutation score while maintaining readability of the test cases. There have been some studies on how to amplify tests made by Google [27] and Facebook [5], which asked the professional developer to generate new tests manually that help in increasing mutation score. The two studies are different to ours, however, as they focus on trying to amplify the tests manually, whereas in the study of this paper, we focus on trying to automate this process.

7 Conclusions and Future Work

Test amplification tools aim to improve developer-written tests, but are limited in the changes they can make and are not guided by fine-grained fitness information.

Search-based test case generation tools like *EvoSuite*, on the other hand, can benefit from the guidance provided by fitness functions, and have a lot more control over the structure of tests, but are limited in terms of their re-use of developer tests and the final readability of the tests they generate.

In this paper, we formulated a version of *EvoSuite*, $EvoSuite_{Amp}$, that uses its carving functionality to start the search on the basis of developer-written test code, and evolves the tests towards killing mutants. When evaluating it against the state-of-the-art Java test amplification tool *DSpot*, $EvoSuite_{Amp}$ was better at killing more mutants and killing more unique mutants that *DSpot* was found to never kill in any of the 30 re-runs of our experiments.

In essence, our paper shows that it is possible for automated tools to kill more mutants when starting from developer-written tests, so long as they are given more flexibility in terms of modifying those tests, as well as adequate guidance. However, the downside is less readability of the final tests, since they are further away from the original ones provided by developers. This suggests two possible alternative avenues for future work. Firstly, test amplification tools like *DSpot* could be improved with finer-grained fitness information, and modified to not throw away tests that are improved with respect to fitness goals—with the intention of further improving them so that they eventually kill more mutants; and/or secondly, tools like *EvoSuite* should be adapted, so they are better at utilizing developer-written tests as a starting point for the search, with the added capability of retaining the characteristics of the original tests, where possible. In particular, work needs to be done in improving *EvoSuite* data structure for encoding tests, so that it can better accommodate the wide variety of styles in which JUnit test cases are written.

References

1. Replication package (2022). https://github.com/test-amplification/EvoSuiteAmp-framework
2. Aniche, M., Treude, C., Zaidman, A.: How developers engineer test cases: an observational study. IEEE Trans. Softw. Eng. (2021). https://ieeexplore.ieee.org/document/9625808
3. Arcuri, A., Briand, L.: A practical guide for using statistical tests to assess randomized algorithms in software engineering. In: 2011 33rd International Conference on Software Engineering (ICSE), pp. 1–10 (2011)
4. Barr, E.T., Harman, M., McMinn, P., Shahbaz, M., Yoo, S.: The oracle problem in software testing: a survey. IEEE Trans. Softw. Eng. **41**(5), 507–525 (2014)
5. Beller, M., et al.: What it would take to use mutation testing in industry-a study at Facebook. In: 2021 IEEE/ACM 43rd International Conference on Software Engineering: Software Engineering in Practice (ICSE-SEIP), pp. 268–277. IEEE (2021)
6. Brandt, C., Zaidman, A.: Developer-centric test amplification. Empir. Softw. Eng. **27**(4), 1–35 (2022). https://doi.org/10.1007/s10664-021-10094-2
7. Coles, H., Laurent, T., Henard, C., Papadakis, M., Ventresque, A.: PIT: a practical mutation testing tool for Java. In: Proceedings of the 25th International Symposium on Software Testing and Analysis, pp. 449–452 (2016)

8. Daka, E., Campos, J., Fraser, G., Dorn, J., Weimer, W.: Modeling readability to improve unit tests. In: Proceedings of the 2015 10th Joint Meeting on Foundations of Software Engineering, pp. 107–118 (2015)
9. Danglot, B., Vera-Perez, O., Yu, Z., Zaidman, A., Monperrus, M., Baudry, B.: A snowballing literature study on test amplification. J. Syst. Softw. **157**, 110398 (2019)
10. Danglot, B., Vera-Pérez, O.L., Baudry, B., Monperrus, M.: Automatic test improvement with DSpot: a study with ten mature open-source projects. Empir. Softw. Eng. **24**(4), 2603–2635 (2019). https://doi.org/10.1007/s10664-019-09692-y
11. DeMillo, R., Lipton, R., Sayward, F.: Hints on test data selection: help for the practicing programmer. Computer **11**(4), 34–41 (1978). https://doi.org/10.1109/C-M.1978.218136
12. Derakhshanfar, P., Devroey, X., Perrouin, G., Zaidman, A., van Deursen, A.: Search-based crash reproduction using behavioural model seeding. Softw. Test. Verif. Reliab. **30**(3), e1733 (2020)
13. Fraser, G., Arcuri, A.: EvoSuite: automatic test suite generation for object-oriented software. In: Proceedings of the 19th ACM SIGSOFT Symposium and the 13th European Conference on Foundations of Software Engineering, pp. 416–419 (2011)
14. Fraser, G., Zeller, A.: Mutation-driven generation of unit tests and oracles. IEEE Trans. Softw. Eng. **38**(2), 278–292 (2011)
15. Geist, R., Offutt, A.J., Harris, F.C.: Estimation and enhancement of real-time software reliability through mutation analysis. IEEE Trans. Comput. **41**(5), 550–558 (1992)
16. Grano, G., Scalabrino, S., Gall, H.C., Oliveto, R.: An empirical investigation on the readability of manual and generated test cases. In: 2018 IEEE/ACM 26th International Conference on Program Comprehension (ICPC), pp. 348–351. IEEE (2018)
17. Jia, Y., Harman, M.: An analysis and survey of the development of mutation testing. IEEE Trans. Softw. Eng. **37**(5), 649–678 (2011)
18. Just, R.: The major mutation framework: efficient and scalable mutation analysis for Java. In: Proceedings of the 2014 International Symposium on Software Testing and Analysis, pp. 433–436 (2014)
19. Just, R., Jalali, D., Ernst, M.D.: Defects4J: a database of existing faults to enable controlled testing studies for Java programs. In: Proceedings of the 2014 International Symposium on Software Testing and Analysis, pp. 437–440 (2014)
20. Kracht, J.S., Petrovic, J.Z., Walcott-Justice, K.R.: Empirically evaluating the quality of automatically generated and manually written test suites. In: 2014 14th International Conference on Quality Software, pp. 256–265. IEEE (2014)
21. McMinn, P.: Search-based software test data generation: a survey. Softw. Test. Verif. Reliab. **14**(2), 105–156 (2004)
22. Nijkamp, N., Brandt, C., Zaidman, A.: Naming amplified tests based on improved coverage. In: 2021 IEEE 21st International Working Conference on Source Code Analysis and Manipulation (SCAM), pp. 237–241 (2021)
23. Olsthoorn, M., Derakhshanfar, P., Devroey, X.: An application of model seeding to search-based unit test generation for Gson. In: Aleti, A., Panichella, A. (eds.) SSBSE 2020. LNCS, vol. 12420, pp. 239–245. Springer, Cham (2020). https://doi.org/10.1007/978-3-030-59762-7_17
24. Oosterbroek, W., Brandt, C., Zaidman, A.: Removing redundant statements in amplified test cases. In: 2021 IEEE 21st International Working Conference on Source Code Analysis and Manipulation (SCAM), pp. 242–246 (2021)

25. Panichella, S., Gambi, A., Zampetti, F., Riccio, V.: SBST tool competition 2021. In: 2021 IEEE/ACM 14th International Workshop on Search-Based Software Testing (SBST), pp. 20–27. IEEE (2021)
26. Parry, O., Hilton, M., Kapfhammer, G.M., McMinn, P.: A survey of flaky tests. ACM Trans. Softw. Eng. Methodol. **31**(1), 1–74 (2022)
27. Petrovic, G., Ivankovic, M., Fraser, G., Just, R.: Practical mutation testing at scale: a view from Google. IEEE Trans. Softw. Eng. **48**(10), 3900–3912 (2022)
28. Rojas, J.M., Fraser, G., Arcuri, A.: Seeding strategies in search-based unit test generation. Softw. Test. Verif. Reliab. **26**(5), 366–401 (2016)
29. Schoofs, E., Abdi, M., Demeyer, S.: AmPyfier: test amplification in Python. arXiv preprint arXiv:2112.11155 (2021)
30. Serra, D., Grano, G., Palomba, F., Ferrucci, F., Gall, H.C., Bacchelli, A.: On the effectiveness of manual and automatic unit test generation: ten years later. In: 2019 IEEE/ACM 16th International Conference on Mining Software Repositories (MSR), pp. 121–125. IEEE (2019)
31. Shamshiri, S., Just, R., Rojas, J.M., Fraser, G., McMinn, P., Arcuri, A.: Do automatically generated unit tests find real faults? An empirical study of effectiveness and challenges (t). In: 2015 30th IEEE/ACM International Conference on Automated Software Engineering (ASE), pp. 201–211 (2015)
32. Yoo, S., Harman, M.: Test data regeneration: generating new test data from existing test data. Softw. Test. Verif. Reliab. **22**(3), 171–201 (2012)

Efficient Fairness Testing Through Hash-Based Sampling

Zhenjiang Zhao[1]([⊠]) [iD], Takahisa Toda[1] [iD], and Takashi Kitamura[2] [iD]

[1] Graduate School of Informatics and Engineering,
University of Electro-Communications, Tokyo, Japan
{zhenjiang,toda}@disc.lab.uec.ac.jp
[2] National Institute of Advanced Industrial Science and Technology (AIST),
Tokyo, Japan
t.kitamura@aist.go.jp

Abstract. There is a growing concern on algorithm fairness, according to wider adoption of machine learning techniques in our daily life. Testing of individual fairness is an approach to algorithm fairness concern. Verification Based Testing (VBT) is a state-of-the-art testing technique for individual fairness, that leverages verification techniques using constraint solving. In this paper, we develop a black-box individual fairness testing technique VBT-X, which applies hash-based sampling techniques to the test case generation part of VBT, aiming to improve its testing ability. Our evaluation by experiments confirms that VBT-X improves the testing ability of VBT by 2.92 times in average.

Keywords: Algorithm fairness · Fairness testing · SAT/SMT solving

1 Introduction

Decision making algorithms based on machine learning (ML) have been more widely adopted in our daily life, in e.g., criminal sentencing [13], financial and insurance [2], hiring [11], (see [19], for more examples). Such algorithmic decision making can overcome some limitations of human decision making, however, there is also a growing concern on fairness of such algorithms, since they tend to be biased, unfairly treating individuals based on sensitive attributes, such as race, gender, and age. For example, COMPAS algorithm, which predicts future criminal, used to determine criminal sentencing, is known to be biased against black defendants [13].

Testing of *individual fairness* is an approach to algorithm fairness concern. *Individual fairness* is a concept of algorithm fairness, which states that an ML classifier should give similar prediction to similar individuals [7]. Testing of individual fairness aims to detect data that violate the concept (called, *discriminatory data*), contained in the given ML classifier under test (CUT). The subject has been studied extensively in previous years, which renders a variety of testing techniques e.g., [1,8,16,23–25,27,28]. These testing techniques respectively use their own search algorithms to generate a set of test cases (i.e., a test set),

M. Papadakis and S. R. Vergilio (Eds.): SSBSE 2022, LNCS 13711, pp. 35–50, 2022.
https://doi.org/10.1007/978-3-031-21251-2_3

which can effectively detect discriminatory data, from the huge input space of the given CUT.

Verification Based Testing (VBT) [24,25], recently developed by Sharma and Wehrheim, is a state-of-the-art black-box testing technique for individual fairness. While VBT detects the presence of discriminatory data in a given CUT, its basic mechanism internally builds a decision tree (DT) classifier represented in SMT (Satisfiability Modulo Theory) constraints as an approximation classifier of CUT, and generates test cases applying SMT solving to the constraints. In the mechanism, a key technical challenge lies on the test generation part, since a technique is required to efficiently search a test set to effectively detect discriminatory data, given the SMT represented DT classifier. VBT proposes two test search techniques, called *data pruning* and *branch pruning*. The more elaborated one, i.e., *branch pruning*, tries to generate diverse test cases by traversing the (SMT-represented) DT, using repetitive calls of SMT solver.

In this paper, we develop an individual fairness testing technique, named VBT-X, by applying the hash-based sampling [3–5,9] in the test generation part of VBT. The hash-based sampling techniques, given a logical formula ϕ, generate diverse solutions of ϕ. Its advantage is the ability to sample diverse solutions at a reasonable computational cost. The techniques have been studied actively, with applications such as probabilistic inference [22], network reliability estimation [6], and verification [18]. Our aim is to leverage its diverse sampling ability in the test generation (i.e., test search) part of VBT, to improve testing ability of VBT. We also devise several enhancement techniques to improve efficiency of VBT-X. Our evaluation confirms that VBT-X achieves a higher testing ability than VBT by 2.92 times in average.

This paper is organized as follows: Sect. 2 reviews the concept of individual fairness, the algorithm of VBT and the hash-based sampling. In Sect. 3, we explain the basic approach of our proposed technique, as Basic VBT-X, and introduce several enhancements to Basic VBT-X, proposing VBT-X. Section 4 is devoted to evaluation of VBT-X by experiments. We discuss related studies in Sect. 5, and mention validity threats of this study in Sect. 6. Section 7 concludes this paper, discussing future work also.

2   Background

This section reviews individual fairness testing (referring to [16]), VBT [27] and hash-based sampling [3–5,9].

2.1   Individual Fairness Testing

Let $P = \{p_1, p_2, \cdots, p_n\}$ be a set of *attributes* (or *parameters*), for $n \in \mathbb{N}$. We use p_i to indicate the i-th attribute in P. Each attribute $p_i \in P$ is associated with a set of *values*, called the *domain* of p_i, denoted by $Dom(p_i)$, such that $(Dom(p_i))_{i \in n}$ is pairwise disjoint. The input space $\mathbb{I}$ of a set of attributes P is the Cartesian product of the domains of $p_1, p_2 \cdots p_n (\in P)$, i.e., $\mathbb{I} = Dom(p_1) \times$

Algorithm 1: VBT algorithm

Data: Classifier (f), Iteration limit ($limit$)
Result: Discriminatory data set (D_{disc})
1 Step-0: Make a training dataset D_{train} with randomly generated data;
2 **repeat**
3   Step-1: Make an approximation f' of CUT f by training a decision tree classifier with D_{train} ;
4   Step-2: Construct SMT constraints $\phi_{f'}$ from approximation f' ;
5   Step-3: Generate test cases by SMT solver;
6   Step-4: Execute test cases against CUT f, to detect discriminatory data;
7   Step-5: Update the training dataset D_{train} with failing test cases;
8 **until** *Iteration exceeds limit* ;

$Dom(p_2) \times \cdots \times Dom(p_n)$. An element I of $\mathbb{I}$ is called a *data item* or *data instance*. We also introduce $P_{prot} \subseteq P$ as the set of protected attributes (e.g., gender, race, age). An ML classifier, whose input space is $\mathbb{I}$, is a function f such that $f(I)$ is the output (i.e., decision) that the classifier f makes for input I.

Definition 1 (Individual discriminatory data and Fairness [27]). *Let ϕ be a classifier under test (CUT), γ be the pre-determined threshold (e.g. chosen by the user), and $I, I' \in \mathbb{I}$. Assume that there exists a non-empty set $Q \subseteq P_{prot}$ s.t. for all $q \in Q$, $I_q \neq I'_q$ and for all $p \in P \backslash Q$, $I_p = I'_p$. If $|f(I) - f(I')| > \gamma$, then I (also I') is called a discriminatory data item of the classifier f, as an instance that manifests the violation of (individual) fairness in f.*

Example 1. Consider an ML classifier f that, taking an individual as input, predicts if the individual gets a loan. Individuals are schemed by three attributes of 'gender', 'income', and 'age', and suppose 'gender' is the protected attribute. Consider the following two individuals I_1 and I_2 that differ only in the protected attribute:

$$I_1 : (gender = male, \quad income = 1000, \ age = 40) \tag{1}$$

$$I_2 : (gender = female, income = 1000, \ age = 40) \tag{2}$$

Suppose the classifier f gives 1 (Yes) to individual I_1, and 0 (No) to I_2; i.e., $f(I_1) = 1$ and $f(I_2) = 0$. Since we have $|f(I_1) - f(I_2)| > \gamma$ assuming $\gamma = 0$, I_1 (and I_2) is a discriminatory data item.

2.2 Verification Based Testing (VBT)

We briefly review the algorithm of VBT, shown in Algorithm 1. VBT takes the classifier under test (CUT) f, and outputs discriminatory data. Details of the internal mechanism are given by steps as follows:

38   Z. Zhao et al.

Step-0: Make a training dataset D_{train} with randomly generated data. This step is executed once at the beginning. The input data instances in D_{train} are generated randomly, and their output labels are obtained by feeding them to CUT f.

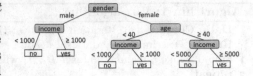

Fig. 1. A decision tree for predicting who gets a loan

Step-1: Make an approximation f' of CUT f by training a decision tree (DT) classifier with D_{train}. For the training in the first iteration, the data set D_{train} created in Step-0 is used. From the second iteration, D_{train} updated in Step-5 is used, where training works as re-training of the approximation f' for refinement. Figure 1 shows an example trained DT (i.e., approximation f').

Step-2: Construct SMT constraints $\phi_{f'}$ from approximation f'. The construction of SMT constraints is designed to check the following: "*Does a discriminatory data instance exist in the given DT?*"

The construction first prepares two variable sequences $x_1^1 \cdots x_1^n$ and $x_2^1 \cdots x_2^n$, where n is the number of attributes and denoted by x_1 and x_2. They express two persons (person 1 and 2) as value assignments for the n variables. Using such variables, the two constraint components '*Unfair*' and '*DecTree*' are built.

The component '*Unfair*' is to check if two persons (x_1, x_2) that are identical except for the protected attribute have different classifier outcomes as follows, where $class_i$ represents the classifier output for individual i:

$$Unfair := \bigwedge_{p \in P \setminus P_{prot}} (x_1^p = x_2^p) \;\&\; \left(\bigvee_{p \in P_{prot}} (x_1^p \neq x_2^p) \right) \;\&\; (class_1 \neq class_2),$$

The component '*DecTree*' specifies that the two persons (x_1, x_2) and classifier's outcomes should conform to the approximation f'. The approximation f' is thus encoded into SMT constrains as follows:

$$DecTree_i(DT) := \bigwedge_{\pi: \, path} \left(\bigwedge_{1 \leq k < |\pi|} \pi.branch(k) \right) \Rightarrow \pi.leaf,$$

where π in the outer conjunction runs over all paths of DT; each conjunct is a predicate of implication form; for the k-th branch node of π, we denote by $\pi.branch(k)$ the (in)equality formula relating the value on an edge to the attribute on the k-th branch node, and by $\pi.leaf$ the (in)equality formula relating the value in the leaf node to the output label.

DT is encoded by conjoining each constraint of two individuals; i.e. $DecTree := DecTree_1 \;\&\; DecTree_2$. The constraint formula $\phi_{f'}$ is constructed as $\phi_{f'} := DecTree \wedge Unfair$. For example, the *DecTree* and *Unfair* constructed from Fig. 1 are respectively expressed in line 1–14 and line 15–17 in Fig. 2.

We can obtain a discriminatory data instance by solving the constraints $\phi_{f'}$; i.e., there exists a discriminatory data instance if the constraint is satisfiable,

```
1   DecTree₁ :
2   (gender₁ = 0)  &  (income₁ < 1000)  ⇒ (class₁ = 0)
3   (gender₁ = 0)  &  (income₁ >= 1000) ⇒ (class₁ = 1)
4   (gender₁ = 1)  &  (age₁ < 40)  &  (income₁ < 1000)  ⇒ (class₁ = 0)
5   (gender₁ = 1)  &  (age₁ < 40)  &  (income₁ >= 1000) ⇒ (class₁ − 1)
6   (gender₁ = 1)  &  (age₁ >= 40) &  (income₁ < 5000)  ⇒ (class₁ = 0)
7   (gender₁ = 1)  &  (age₁ >= 40) &  (income₁ >= 5000) ⇒ (class₁ = 1)
8   DecTree₂ :
9   (gender₂ = 0)  &  (income₂ < 1000)  ⇒ (class₂ = 0)
10  (gender₂ = 0)  &  (income₂ >= 1000) ⇒ (class₂ = 1)
11  (gender₂ = 1)  &  (age₂ < 40)  &  (income₂ < 1000)  ⇒ (class₂ = 0)
12  (gender₂ = 1)  &  (age₂ < 40)  &  (income₂ >= 1000) ⇒ (class₂ = 1)
13  (gender₂ = 1)  &  (age₂ >= 40) &  (income₂ < 5000)  ⇒ (class₂ = 0)
14  (gender₂ = 1)  &  (age₂ >= 40) &  (income₂ >= 5000) ⇒ (class₂ = 1)
15  Unfair :
16  (gender₁ ≠ gender₂)  &  (income₁ = income₂)  &  (age₁ = age₂)
17  (class₁ ≠ class₂)
```

Fig. 2. SMT formula used for test case generation

and such an instance can be retrieved from the solution, which is given as a value assignment for the variables in $\phi_{f'}$. For example, the set of the constraints in Fig. 2 is satisfiable. We can thus retrieve the value assignment for two persons (x_1, x_2) and their outcome of classifier from the solution below. Observe that x_1 (and x_2) is a discriminatory data instance for approximation classifier f'.

$$x_1 : [gender_1 = 0, income_1 = 1000, age_1 = 40, class_1 = 1]$$
$$x_2 : [gender_2 = 1, income_2 = 1000, age_2 = 40, class_2 = 0]$$

Step-3: Generate test cases by SMT solver. This step generates numerous test cases using SMT constraints $\phi_{f'}$ constructed in Step-2. VBT uses data instances satisfying $\phi_{f'}$ (i.e., discriminatory data in the approximation f') as test cases. This is based on the idea that discriminatory data in an approximation f' is likely to be one in CUT f, too.

A technical difficulty here arises on how to generate as many test cases as we want using the SMT constraints $\phi_{f'}$. VBT realizes it by two kinds of technique, called *data pruning* and *branch pruning*. The data pruning generates test cases by repeatedly solving the constraints $\phi_{f'}$, while adding blocking clauses in each iteration to block regenerating the test cases that have been generated so far. The branch pruning generates test cases by traversing paths of the DT. It generates a maximum of $2k$ test cases for a DT with k hight (i.e., k attributes) (Algorithm 3 of [25]). Appropriate clauses are added to $\phi_{f'}$ to guide traversing the DT. Test cases are generated by repeatedly solving such constraints.

Step-4: Execute test cases against CUT f to detect discriminatory data. Not all test cases (i.e., discriminatory data in the approximation f') are necessarily discriminatory data in CUT f^1. Test cases are thus actually tested against f.

---

[1] Test cases are thus also called *candidates* in [24].

We distinguish success test cases, which are actually discriminatory data for f, from failing ones, which are not.

Step-5: Update the training dataset by adding failing test cases. Failing test cases represent points where the approximated classifier f' differs from CUT f. VBT accumulates such failing test cases in D_{train} for re-training the approximation f' for refinement in Step-1 in the next iteration. By repeatedly refining f', VBT more efficiently detects discriminatory data.

2.3   Hash-Based Sampling

Overview. The concept of hash-based sampling techniques of Boolean formula F is to randomly divide the input space of F (denoted by, $\{0,1\}^n$, where n is the number of variables in F) into "small cells" of roughly equal size, and to pick a solution from one such cell. The partition of the input space is virtually done by determining a random hash function $h\colon \{0,1\}^n \to \{0,1,\ldots,m-1\}$, where let m be the number of cells, so that the inverse images $h^{-1}(0),\ldots,h^{-1}(m-1)$ correspond to the partitioned cells.

A common practice to realize this is to impose random *XOR clauses* on F. Here, an XOR clause is a formula constructed from Boolean variables or constants $(0,1)$ using XOR operators. XOR clauses have effect of restricting the solution space (i.e., the set of all solutions of F) to one randomly chosen cell. Since imposing a single XOR clause on F means roughly halving the solution space of F (and selecting one of them), imposing s XOR clauses means dividing the solution space into 2^s cells of roughly equal size (and selecting one of them). A solution is sampled by applying an off-the-shelf solver to the resulted formula, i.e., the conjunction of XOR clauses and F. We repeat this procedure but with fresh XOR clauses in each repetition, to generate as many samples as we need.

Hash-Based Sampling by Gomes et al. Since the invention of the hash-based sampling by Sipser [26], a variety of techniques for it have been investigated [3–5, 9]. Among them, we review the technique XORSAMPLE by Gomes et al. [9], which captures the essence of the hash-based sampling and is easy to apply and implement in the VBT approach.

Algorithm 2: XORSAMPLE

Parameter : $q \in (0,1)$, a positive integer s
Data: A satisfiable propositional formula F
Result: A solution of F

1 **while** *True* **do**
2 | $G \leftarrow s$ XOR clauses, each variable chosen with probability q and the constant 1 with $1/2$;
3 | **if** *F & G is satisfiable* **then**
4 | | $\sigma \leftarrow GetSolution(F$ & $G)$;
5 | | **if** *there is no other solution* **then**
    | | | **return** σ ;

Algorithm 2 shows the algorithm of XORSAMPLE [9]. The steps in each iteration are: Generate XOR clauses (G) so that each clause selects each variable in F with probability q and the constant 1 with probability $1/2$; Find a solution for the conjunction of F and G by applying a generic solver; If a solution σ is found, then find another solution[2] except σ; If it is confirmed that there is no other solution, return σ, and otherwise go to the next iteration. The former case means that σ is a unique solution for $F \wedge G$, i.e., the cell is enough "small". The algorithm terminates only if this case happens.

3 Proposed Method

In this section, we develop VBT-X, a method of integrating the hash-based sampling with VBT. Its basic idea is to apply the essence of the hash-based sampling (explained in Sect. 2.3) to the test generation part (Step-3) of the VBT algorithm (Algorithm 1). The development is presented in two-steps. We first develop the basic method as 'Basic VBT-X' in Sect. 3.1, and next develop several enhancement techniques, presenting 'VBT-X' in Sect. 3.2.

3.1 Basic Method (Basic VBT-X)

Introducing Auxiliary Variables. The first difficulty we encounter in applying the hash-based sampling to VBT is that the variables in SMT constraints are inherently non-binary, i.e., their domains are often integers and real values. Take, for instance, the constraint at line 2 in Fig. 2:

$$(gender_1 = 0) \wedge (income_1 < 1000) \Rightarrow (class_1 = 0). \tag{3}$$

The variable $income_1$ is real-valued, although $gender_1$ and $class_1$ happen to be binary in the current case. In general, the input space of SMT constraints is the Cartesian product of the domains of multi-valued variables. In order to adapt the hash-based sampling to this setup, we need to somehow consider dividing this space into small cells.

To resolve this issue, we introduce auxiliary Boolean variables, called *sampling variables* (denoted by $z_1, z_2, \cdots$), for the node constraints in *DecTree*, and *sampling constraints* that assign the node constraints to the sampling variables using the logical equivalence relation. Based on the setting, we impose random XOR clauses over those sampling variables on an SMT formula, simulating Algorithm 2.

For example, for constraint (3), we introduce the two sampling variables, z_1 and z_3, and two sampling constraints $z_1 \Leftrightarrow (gender_1 = 0)$ and $z_3 \Leftrightarrow (income_1 < 1000)$. Suppose here a single XOR clause, say $z_1 \oplus z_3$, happens to be imposed. Because of the sampling constraints to z_1 and z_3, the effect is that one of $(gender_1 = 0)$ and $(income_1 < 1000)$ is true, but not both of them, and the input space is partitioned into two: one satisfying $z_1 \oplus z_3$ and the other. It is thus expected that random XOR clauses introduced as above bring similar effect as in XORSAMPLE to our SMT setup.

---

[2] One more run of the solver is sufficient to do this, but we omit the details due to the space limitation.

42   Z. Zhao et al.

Automatically Deciding the Number of XOR Clauses (s). To fully automate the testing process of the proposed technique, we decide the number of
XOR clauses (s) in the following way: increment s from 0 to 20 until for s XOR
clauses (G) randomly generated as in line 1, the formula ϕ'_f & I & G becomes
unsatisfiable; let the final value for s be multiplied by 0.5.

Basic Test Case Generation Using XOR Sampling. Based on the prepara-
tion explained in Sect. 3.1, Algorithm 3 shows the basic test generation algorithm
of our proposed method. The steps are: Introduce sampling variables for all node
constraints in *DecTree* and generate the sampling constraints for them (line 1).
For instance, the sampling constraints for the SMT formula in Fig. 2 are listed
in Fig. 3. Next, estimate the parameter s as explained in Sect. 3.1. In the while
loop, generate XOR clauses (G) each time; find a solution for ϕ'_f & I & G, if
exists, by applying an SMT solver; accumulate it.

Remark. We remark
that (1) the heuristic
search (in Sect. 3.1)
is ad-hoc and (2)
checking of unique
solutions (in line 5
of Algorithm 2) is
skipped in Algorithm
3. These may affect
the degree of unifor-
mity, but there are
several reasons for the
design choices. First,
we find it technically
difficult to determine
optimal s as well as

Algorithm 3: Test case generation by XOR constraints

Parameter : $q \in (0,1)$
Data: A positive integer k, a satisfiable SMT formula
$\phi_{f'} = DecTree \wedge Unfair$
Result: k (possibly duplicate) solutions of $\phi_{f'}$
1 $I \leftarrow$ Sampling constraints;
2 $s \leftarrow$ estimated the number of XOR clauses
   // Section 3.1
3 $Sol \leftarrow \emptyset$ // multiset
4 **while** $|Sol| < k$ **do**
5 $\quad G \leftarrow s$ XOR clauses, each sampling variable
      chosen with probability q, constant 1 with 1/2;
6 $\quad$ **if** $\phi_{f'}$ & I & G *is satisfiable* **then**
      $Sol \leftarrow Sol \cup GetSolution(\phi_{f'}$ & I & $G)$;
7 **return** Sol;

---

make solutions unique. Second, the proposed method performs better than VBT
even with the ad-hoc search and without the uniqueness checking, as will be
shown in Sect. 4, which accomplishes our purpose. Third, modern techniques
(e.g., [3–5]) in SAT solving use different techniques, such as independent supports and solution enumeration (BSAT), instead of considering uniqueness of
solutions, and they not only lead to large performance gain but also provide
a theoretical guarantee of almost-uniformity, which we are more interested in
employing but it seems to cause unacceptable overhead if those techniques are
simulated in our SMT setup in a straightforward way.

3.2   Enhancement (VBT-X)

Reducing Sampling Variables. Properly determining sampling variables to be used affects the degree of uniformity as well as time required for sampling. We present three ways of reducing sampling variables. The first two leverage the notion of *independent supports*, and we begin with reviewing it.

$z_1 \Leftrightarrow (gender_1 = 0)$ $z_9 \Leftrightarrow (gender_2 = 0)$

$z_2 \Leftrightarrow (gender_1 = 1)$ $z_{10} \Leftrightarrow (gender_2 = 1)$

$z_3 \Leftrightarrow (income_1 < 1000)$ $z_{11} \Leftrightarrow (income_2 < 1000)$

$z_4 \Leftrightarrow (income_1 >= 1000)$ $z_{12} \Leftrightarrow (income_2 >= 1000)$

$z_5 \Leftrightarrow (income_1 < 5000)$ $z_{13} \Leftrightarrow (income_2 < 5000)$

$z_6 \Leftrightarrow (income_1 >= 5000)$ $z_{14} \Leftrightarrow (income_2 >= 5000)$

$z_7 \Leftrightarrow (age_1 < 40)$ $z_{15} \Leftrightarrow (age_2 < 40)$

$z_8 \Leftrightarrow (age_1 >= 40)$ $z_{16} \Leftrightarrow (age_2 >= 40)$

Fig. 3. Sampling constraints of the basic version

Independent Support. Independent support of Boolean formula F [12] is a subset of variables in F such that in every solution of F, the truth values of these variables determine those of the other variables. In the hash-based sampling, it is desirable to focus on as a small independent support as possible and perform sampling by generating XOR clauses over independent support only. This is because XOR clauses have to decouple the dependency between variables in the independent support; if XOR clauses included many other variables, they would bring bias in such a way that the truth values of some variables in drawn samples were unfairly tied. What is worse, it is extremely hard to find a solution of F constrained by long XOR clauses. We will thus consider variables that turn out, from the VBT setup, to have the dependency in their truth values.

Equivalence. Because of the unfairness constraint *Unfair*, some pairs of SMT variables having common non-protected attributes, say age_1 and age_2, must have the same value. Hence, from the following two sampling constraints, the sampling variables z_7 and z_{15} must be logically equivalent: $z_7 \Leftrightarrow (age_1 < 40)$ and $z_{15} \Leftrightarrow (age_2 < 40)$. Clearly, it is sufficient to consider only one of them, say z_7, to be included in XOR clauses, and introduce only the sampling constraint for the variable considered: $z_7 \Leftrightarrow (age_1 < 40)$.

Exclusive OR. Consider the following constraints: $z_7 \Leftrightarrow (age_1 < 40)$ $z_8 \Leftrightarrow (age_1 >= 40)$. Clearly, one of $(age_1 < 40)$ and $(age_1 >= 40)$, is true, but not both of them; the same applies to their sampling variables z_7 and z_8. Hence, it is sufficient to consider only one of z_7 and z_8 to be included in XOR clauses, and introduce only the sampling constraint for it.

Symmetry. Suppose we have a solution σ for the SMT constraints in Fig. 2, that induces the following discriminatory data instance x_1 (and x_2):

$x_1:$ $[gender_1 = 0, income_1 = 1000, age_1 = 40, class_1 = 1]$

$x_2:$ $[gender_2 = 1, income_2 = 1000, age_2 = 40, class_2 = 0]$

The following assignment σ', obtained from σ by swapping x_1 and x_2, is also satisfying the constraints.

$$x_1' : \qquad [gender_1 = 1, income_1 = 1000, age_1 = 40, class_1 = 0]$$
$$x_2' : \qquad [gender_2 = 0, income_2 = 1000, age_2 = 40, class_2 = 1]$$

This symmetry holds in general because of the construction of *Unfair* and *DecTree*. That is, for any solution σ of $\phi_f' = DecTree$ & *Unfair* for x_1 and x_2, the assignment, σ', obtained from σ by swapping x_1 and x_2 is also satisfying. The truth values of sampling variables differ only in those of the protected attribute, i.e., *gender* in the above case. We do not want to distinguish σ and σ'. We hence do not include all sampling variables of the protected attribute in XOR clauses, and do not introduce the sampling constraints for them. For the running example, the followings are ignored: $z_1 \Leftrightarrow (gender_1 = 0)$, $z_2 \Leftrightarrow (gender_1 = 1)$, $z_9 \Leftrightarrow (gender_2 = 0)$, and $z_{10} \Leftrightarrow (gender_2 = 1)$.

Figure 4 lists all sampling constraints for the version in which all variable reductions are applied.

Shortening XOR Clause Length. As mentioned in Sect. 3.2, short XOR clauses are preferable in practice. The variable reductions given so far are effective for shortening XOR clause length because the expected length is determined by the number of sampling variables and the probability with which each variable is chosen.

We here present another way, which is expected to not sacrifice the degree of uniformity so much. In order to build an XOR clause, for each attribute we randomly choose one from the sampling variables having the attribute in common and determine with given probability q whether or not it is included in the current XOR clause. For

$z_3 \Leftrightarrow (income_1 < 1000)$

$z_5 \Leftrightarrow (income_1 < 5000)$

$z_7 \Leftrightarrow (age_1 < 40)$

Fig. 4. Sampling constraints of the improved version

instance, we have three sampling variables z_3, z_5, z_7 in Fig. 4. Since z_3 and z_5 have the same attribute *income*, we choose one of z_3 and z_5 at random, and then determine with probability q whether or not it is included. Clearly, the expected length of an XOR clause is related to the number of non-protected attributes.

4   Evaluation

This section reports our evaluation of the proposed technique by experiments.

For evaluation, we set the following two RQs.

RQ1: Can VBT-X detect discriminatory data more efficiently than VBT?

RQ2: Are the enhancement techniques of VBT-X effective?

RQ1 is the main RQ, since efficient detection of discriminatory data is the main motivation of this work, like other algorithm development for individual fairness testing [1,8,24]. In addition, recall that our work is motivated to improve the VBT framework, which is shown to perform better than other main black-box testing approaches in [24]. RQ2 quantitatively evaluates performance improvement brought by the enhancement techniques explained in Sect. 3.2.

4.1 Experimental Setup

For experiments to run VBT, we use the VBT implementation[3] by the authors of [24]. For all experiments, we use VBT branch pruning for test generation strategy, instead of data pruning, since it is shown in [24] that branch pruning is more efficient. We have implemented the basic version and the improved version of VBT-X (which are respetively called 'Basic VBT-X' and just 'VBT-X'), using Python version 3.8.10 and Scikit-learn version 0.22.1, modifying the original VBT implementation. For a fair comparison, we use the same setup regarding classifiers, datasets, and protected attributes as in [24], which render 16 (= $4 \times 2 \times 2$) configurations, as follows:

- Classifier: Logistic Regression (LR), Random Forest (RF), Naive Bayes (NB), Decision Tree (DT)
- Dataset: 'Adult' Census Income[4], 'German' Credit Card[5]
- Protected attribute: Gender (Male, Female), Race (White, others), Age

For RQ1, we compare the numbers of detected discriminatory data by VBT and VBT-X within a given execution time limit. We also investigate the cause of the result. We specifically investigate two possibilities for it: the result is mainly caused by difference in (1) the numbers of generated (and hence executed) test cases, and/or (2) precision scores (i.e., hit ratios of discriminatory data over generated test cases) of VBT and VBT-X.

For RQ2, instead of using the heuristic search to decide the number of clauses s explained in Sect. 3.1, we compare Basic VBT-X and VBT-X by executing them with $s = 10$. This is because Basic VBT-X with automatic decision of s runs too slow to detect any discriminatory data for most of the configurations, within our execution time limit. We also investigate the cause of the result, similarly to RQ1. We thus measure (1) numbers of generated test cases, and (2) precision scores of Basic VBT-X and VBT-X.

For all experiments, we set ten minutes (600 s) for the execution time limit. For each configuration, we execute 10 trials and take the average of them. Intel(R) Xeon(R) Silver 4210 CPU @ 2.20 GHz Processor, 32 GB memory, running Ubuntu 20.04.4 LTS.

---

[3] https://github.com/arnabsharma91/fairCheck.

[4] https://archive.ics.uci.edu/ml/datasets/adult.

[5] https://archive.ics.uci.edu/ml/datasets/statlog+(german+credit+data).

Table 1. The results of experiments. The rows represent configurations, each combined from datasets, classifiers, and Protected features. The columns for 'VBT' and the two versions of 'VBT-X' respectively represent the results of three criteria of the numbers of detected discriminatory data ('#Disc'), the number of generated test cases ('#Tests'), and precision scores ('Prec.'), while their improvement ratios are shown in the next columns (for 'Improvement ratio'). The columns for 'Basic VBT-X (s = 10)' and 'Imp. VBT-X (s = 10)' represent those for Basic VBT-X and Improved VBT-X with $s = 10$, appended with their improvement ratios in the next columns. The bottom row 'avg./total' shows the total numbers (for '#Disc' and '#Test') or averages (for 'Prec.'); and the row '#wins' shows the numbers of configurations that the technique in the column outperforms the competitor in the respective three criteria.

No.	Dataset	Clf.	Prot. feature	VBT			Imp. VBT-X (s: auto)			Improvement ratio			Basic VBT-X (s = 10)			Imp. VBT-X (s = 10)			Improvement ratio		
				#Disc	#Tests	Prec.	#Disc	#Tests	Prec.	#Disc	#Tests	Prec.	#Disc	#Tests	Prec.	#Disc	#Tests	Prec.	#Disc	#Tests	Prec.
1	Adult	LR	Gender	15	269	0.06	28	735	0.04	1.87	2.73	0.67	28	750	0.04	86	2015	0.04	3.07	2.69	1.00
2		LR	Race	69	1864	0.04	52	2145	0.03	0.75	1.15	0.75	72	2365	0.03	91	4015	0.02	1.26	1.70	0.67
3		RF	Gender	728	2161	0.34	1545	2925	0.53	2.12	1.35	1.56	1236	1950	0.63	1878	3475	0.54	1.52	1.78	0.86
4		RF	Race	10	1896	0.006	110	2845	0.04	11.00	1.50	6.67	38	1980	0.02	86	3300	0.03	2.26	1.67	1.50
5		NB	Gender	1669	3329	0.5	4580	5865	0.78	2.74	1.76	1.56	2233	4165	0.54	5033	6645	0.76	2.25	1.60	1.41
6		NB	Race	784	3822	0.21	3837	5635	0.68	4.89	1.47	3.24	1780	4120	0.43	3908	6170	0.63	2.20	1.50	1.47
7		DT	Gender	1688	2127	0.79	5075	5685	0.89	3.01	2.67	1.13	2784	3580	0.78	5777	6600	0.88	2.08	1.84	1.13
8		DT	Race	1748	2531	0.69	5225	5960	0.88	2.99	2.35	1.28	1844	3265	0.57	5040	6325	0.80	2.73	1.94	1.40
9	German	LR	Gender	214	1772	0.12	244	2205	0.11	1.14	1.24	0.92	230	2065	0.11	324	2875	0.11	1.41	1.39	1.00
10		LR	Age	173	1879	0.09	289	2615	0.11	1.67	1.39	1.22	307	2200	0.14	328	2990	0.11	1.07	1.36	0.79
11		RF	Gender	168	1269	0.13	92	1805	0.05	0.55	1.42	0.38	89	1545	0.06	111	2175	0.05	1.25	1.41	0.83
12		RF	Age	66	1286	0.05	116	1870	0.06	1.76	1.45	1.20	125	1615	0.08	129	2180	0.06	1.03	1.35	0.75
13		NB	Gender	77	1297	0.06	82	1850	0.04	1.06	1.43	0.67	70	1605	0.04	127	2535	0.05	1.81	1.58	1.25
14		NB	Age	165	2674	0.06	518	3245	0.16	3.14	1.21	2.67	421	2820	0.15	523	3695	0.14	1.24	1.31	0.93
15		DT	Gender	1343	2403	0.56	3942	4440	0.89	2.94	1.85	1.59	1770	3085	0.57	3519	5060	0.70	1.99	1.64	1.23
16		DT	Age	1081	2471	0.44	3505	4380	0.80	3.24	1.77	1.82	1930	3185	0.60	3109	4955	0.63	1.61	1.56	1.05
			avg./total	9998	33050	0.26	29249	54205	0.38	2.92	1.64	1.47	14957	40295	0.30	30069	65010	0.35	2.01	1.61	1.16
			#wins	2	0	5	14	16	11	N/A	N/A	N/A	0	0	6	16	16	8	N/A	N/A	N/A

4.2   Results

Table 1 shows the results of experiments, based on which we answer the RQs.

RQ1: Can VBT-X detect more discriminatory data than VBT? From the columns for #Disc of VBT and VBT-X in Table 1, we can observe that VBT-X detects more discriminatory data than VBT, by around 2.92 times in average, for 14 out of 16 configurations, and by upto 11 times for configuration No. 4.

From the columns for '#Tests' and 'Prec.' of VBT, VBT-X and their 'Improvement ratio', we can observe the following: (1) VBT-X generates more test cases than VBT by 1.64 times in average and for all the 16 configurations, and (2) the precision of VBT-X is higher than that of VBT by 1.47 times in average and for 11 out of 16 configurations. We thus may be able to ascribe the above conclusion to both of the number of generated test cases and precision scores.

However, with a finer analysis, we can more likely ascribe the conclusion to the number of generated test cases than the precision score. First, we can say that the improvement in the number of generated test cases (1.64) of VBT-X is higher than that of precision score (1.47). Second, VBT-X wins VBT for all the 16 configurations in the number of test cases, but only for 11 configurations in the precision score. Third, for several configurations (No. 1, 9, 13), although precision score of VBT-X is lower than that of VBT, VBT-X can find more discriminatory data since it generates more test cases.

Answer for RQ1: Yes. VBT-X can detect more discriminatory data than VBT by 2.92 times in average and for more than 87 (= 14/16) % configurations.

RQ2: Are the enhancement techniques of VBT-X effective? From the columns for '#Disc' of 'Basic VBT-X(s = 10)' and 'Imp. VBT-X (s = 10)', we can observe that VBT-X detects more discriminatory data than Basic VBT-X by 2.01 times in average and for all the 16 configurations.

From the columns for '#Tests' and 'Prec.' of Basic VBT-X, VBT-X, and their 'Improvement ratio', we can observe that (1) VBT-X generates more test cases than Basic VBT-X by 1.61 times in average and for all the 16 configurations, and (2) the precision score of VBT-X is higher than that of Basic VBT-X by 1.16 times in average and for 8 out of 16 configurations, while Basic VBT-X wins for 6 configurations. We may ascribe the above conclusion to that VBT-X can generate more test cases, since the improvement on precision score may not be enough significant.

Answer for RQ2: Yes, enhancement techniques explained in Sect. 3.2 are effective, as they improve discriminatory-detecting ability of Basic VBT-X by 2.01 times in average.

---

5 Related Work

Testing of individual fairness is first tackled by Galhotra et al. in [8]. The main contribution is establishing its concept, including the concepts of similarity of individuals and discriminatory data, which are explained in Sect. 2.1. The concept has become the basis of most existing studies of individual fairness testing, including our study. They also develop a black-box testing algorithm for this concept, named THEMIS, which detects discriminatory data, given a classifier as input.

Udeshi et al. [27] proposed an efficient black-box testing algorithm for individual fairness, improving the algorithm by Galhotra et al. [8], The algorithm enhances efficiency, by structuring it into two steps of global and local search. This two-step structure of the algorithm leverages robustness of ML classifiers.

Another well-known technique for individual fairness testing is SG [1], featured with its efficient testing ability. Its mechanism is similar to VBT, as it internally builds an approximation classifier of the CUT using a decision tree, and apply symbolic execution using SMT solver to generates test cases. However, VBT differs from SG in many details. E.g., SG approximates the CUT in a partial decision tree using local model explainer (LIME [21]), while VBT do so in an entire decision tree using training. Our work applies hash-based sampling technique to VBT, because it is reported that VBT has a higher testing ability than SG [24]; however, our proposed technique is basically applicable to SG, too.

Sharma and Wehrheim developed VBT originally for testing *monotonicity* of ML classifiers [25], which is similar but different concept from individual fairness.

After extend the work [25] to fairness testing as VBT in [24], they further extend VBT in several respects, as a technique called MLCHECK [23]. An extension is to apply other properties than monotonicity and fairness, such as security. Another direction is to use Relu-based Deep Neural Network, (instead of using decision trees,) for making approximation classifier of classifier under test.

Several other recent studies on black-box individual fairness testing are as follows: A technique developed by Morales et al. [16] (CGFT) improves efficacy of AEQUITAS, by applying combinatorial t-way testing (CT) [14] to the global search of AEQUITAS. Patel et al. [20] investigates efficacy of applying combination of CT and a counterfactual explanation technique, called DICE[17].

Although above-mentioned techniques all take the black-box (a. k. a.,, model-agnostic) testing approach, the algorithm proposed by Zhang et al. [28] takes a white-box approach, targeting Deep Neural Networks (DNNs). The algorithm, named Adversarial Discrimination Finder (ADF), employs adversarial sample generation techniques using gradient analysis [10,15]. Although ADF can be only applicable for DNN-based classifiers, their experiments show ADF finds more discriminatory data than AEQUITAS and SG.

6 Validity Threats

Our experiments use two datasets ('Adult' and 'German'), the four classifiers (LR, RF, NB, DT), and two attributes ('Gender' and 'Race'), which are exactly the same as those used in [24]. There are other datasets available in algorithm fairness literature (see e.g., the survey of [19]), countless kinds of classifiers, and more kinds of protected attributes (such as age, nationality). However, it is practically infeasible to experiments all combinations, due to combination explosions. Experiments in most of other studies on fairness testing [8,16,24,27] thus also use two or three datasets, classifiers, and attributes.

VBT-X inherently contains random behaviours, as it samples different data on different executions. This threat is mitigated by taking average over 10 trials for all experiments. In experiments for RQ2, we use $s = 10$ for the number of XOR clauses s for a conservative evaluation, since Basic VBT-X best performs with $s = 10$ by preliminary experiments with $s = 5, 10, 15$. Our experiments use 10 min (600 s) for the execution timeout limit. There is no standard criteria for execution time limit in fairness testing literature, but more studies seem to use several hundred seconds for it; e.g., [24] uses 930 s and [28] uses 500 s. Our timeout setting follows this convention.

7 Conclusion and Future Work

In this paper, we developed a black box testing technique for individual fairness VBT-X, by applying hash-based sampling techniques [3–5,9] to the test generation of VBT, a state-of-the-art fairness testing technique by Sharma and Wehrheim [24,25]. The novelty of this work is to show the mechanism to apply hash-based sampling, which substantially different approach from VBT, actually works, and performs better than VBT.

There are several directions for future work. One direction is to refine our ad-hoc heuristic search to decide the number of XOR clauses, and improve the degree of uniformity of sampled data in VBT-X, as mentioned in Sect. 7. Several related techniques proposed in SAT solving settings [3–5] may be applicable for the purpose, although we may encounter difficulty to adapt them to our SMT setting. Another direction in the technical side is to apply our proposed technique to MLCHECK [23], which uses Deep Nueral Network (DNN) for approximation classifiers in VBT framework, instead of decision trees. We are also interested in applying VBT-X to other properties such as security (e.g., Trojan attack) than fairness as in [23]. The fourth direction is to conduct more thorough experiments to evaluate our proposed techniques using more datasets, classifiers, and protected attributes to generalize obtained results, as explained in Sect. 6.

Acknowledgements. This paper is partly based on results obtained from a project, JPNP20006, commissioned by the New Energy and Industrial Technology Development Organization (NEDO). We are also indebted to the suggestions from peer reviewers of SSBSE22. Although part of provided suggestions has not been adopted due to limited pages, we intend to incorporate these valuable suggestions in the following research.

References

1. Aggarwal, A., Lohia, P., Nagar, S., Dey, K., Saha, D.: Black box fairness testing of machine learning models. In: Proceedings of ESEC/SIGSOFT FSE, pp. 625–635 (2019)
2. Byanjankar, A., Heikkilä, M., Mezei, J.: Predicting credit risk in peer-to-peer lending: a neural network approach. In: Proceedings of SSCI 2015, pp. 719–725. IEEE (2015)
3. Chakraborty, S., Fremont, D.J., Meel, K.S., Seshia, S.A., Vardi, M.Y.: On parallel scalable uniform SAT witness generation. In: Baier, C., Tinelli, C. (eds.) TACAS 2015. LNCS, vol. 9035, pp. 304–319. Springer, Heidelberg (2015). https://doi.org/10.1007/978-3-662-46681-0_25
4. Chakraborty, S., Meel, K.S., Vardi, M.Y.: A scalable and nearly uniform generator of SAT witnesses. In: Sharygina, N., Veith, H. (eds.) CAV 2013. LNCS, vol. 8044, pp. 608–623. Springer, Heidelberg (2013). https://doi.org/10.1007/978-3-642-39799-8_40
5. Chakraborty, S., Meel, K.S., Vardi, M.Y.: Balancing scalability and uniformity in SAT witness generator. In: Proceedings of DAC 2014, DAC 2014, pp. 1–6 (2014)
6. Duenas-Osorio, L., Meel, K., Paredes, R., Vardi, M.: Counting-based reliability estimation for power-transmission grids. In: Proceedings of AAAI 2017, vol. 31, no. 1, February 2017
7. Dwork, C., Hardt, M., Pitassi, T., Reingold, O., Zemel, R.: Fairness through awareness. In: Proceedings of ITCS 2012, pp. 214–226 (2012)
8. Galhotra, S., Brun, Y., Meliou, A.: Fairness testing: testing software for discrimination. In: Proceedings of ESEC/FSE 2017, pp. 498–510 (2017)
9. Gomes, C.P., Sabharwal, A., Selman, B.: Near-uniform sampling of combinatorial spaces using XOR constraints. In: Proceedings of NIPS 2006, pp. 481–488 (2006)

10. Goodfellow, I.J., Shlens, J., Szegedy, C.: Explaining and harnessing adversarial examples. In: Proceedings of ICLR (2015)
11. Hoffman, M., Kahn, L., Li, D.: Discretion in hiring. Q. J. Econ. **133**(2), 765–800 (2018)
12. Ivrii, A., Malik, S., Meel, K.S., Vardi, M.Y.: On computing minimal independent support and its applications to sampling and counting. Constraints **21**(1), 41–58 (2016). https://doi.org/10.1007/s10601-015-9204-z
13. Angwin, J., Larson, J., Mattu, S., Kirchner, L.: Machine bias (2016). https://www.propublica.org/article/machine-bias-risk-assessments-in-criminal-sentencing
14. Kuhn, R., Kacker, R.: Introduction to Combinatorial Testing. Chapman & Hall CRC (2013)
15. Kurakin, A., Goodfellow, I.J., Bengio, S.: Adversarial examples in the physical world. In: Proceedings of ICLR 2017. OpenReview.net (2017)
16. Perez Morales, D., Kitamura, T., Takada, S.: Coverage-guided fairness testing. In: Lee, R. (ed.) ICIS 2021. SCI, vol. 985, pp. 183–199. Springer, Cham (2021). https://doi.org/10.1007/978-3-030-79474-3_13
17. Mothilal, R.K., Sharma, A., Tan, C.: Explaining machine learning classifiers through diverse counterfactual explanations. In: Proceedings of FACCT 2020, pp. 607–617. ACM (2020)
18. Naveh, Y., et al.: Constraint-based random stimuli generation for hardware verification. In: Proceedings of IAAI 2006, pp. 1720–1727. AAAI Press (2006)
19. Oneto, L., Chiappa, S.: Fairness in machine learning. In: Oneto, L., Navarin, N., Sperduti, A., Anguita, D. (eds.) Recent Trends in Learning From Data. SCI, vol. 896, pp. 155–196. Springer, Cham (2020). https://doi.org/10.1007/978-3-030-43883-8_7
20. Patel, A.R., Chandrasekaran, J., Lei, Y., Kacker, R.N., Kuhn, D.R.: A combinatorial approach to fairness testing of machine learning models. In: Proceedings of IWCT 2022, pp. 1135–1144. IEEE (2022)
21. Ribeiro, M.T., Singh, S., Guestrin, C.: "why should I trust you?": Explaining the predictions of any classifier. In: Proceedings of KDD 2016, pp. 1135–1144. ACM (2016)
22. Roth, D.: On the hardness of approximate reasoning. Artif. Intell. **82**(1), 273–302 (1996)
23. Sharma, A., Demir, C., Ngomo, A.N., Wehrheim, H.: MLCHECK-property-driven testing of machine learning classifiers. In: Proceedings of ICMLA 2021, pp. 738–745 (2021)
24. Sharma, A., Wehrheim, H.: Automatic fairness testing of machine learning models. In: Casola, V., De Benedictis, A., Rak, M. (eds.) ICTSS 2020. LNCS, vol. 12543, pp. 255–271. Springer, Cham (2020). https://doi.org/10.1007/978-3-030-64881-7_16
25. Sharma, A., Wehrheim, H.: Higher income, larger loan? Monotonicity testing of machine learning models. In: Proceedings of ISSTA 2020, pp. 200–210. ACM (2020)
26. Sipser, M.: A complexity theoretic approach to randomness. In: Proceedings of STOC 1983, pp. 330–335. ACM (1983)
27. Udeshi, S., Arora, P., Chattopadhyay, S.: Automated directed fairness testing. In: Proceedings of ASE 2018, pp. 98–108 (2018)
28. Zhang, P., et al.: White-box fairness testing through adversarial sampling. In: Proceedings of ICSE 2020, pp. 949–960 (2020)

Improving Search-Based Android Test Generation Using Surrogate Models

Michael Auer, Felix Adler, and Gordon Fraser[✉]

University of Passau, Passau, Germany
M.Auer@uni-passau.de, adler08@ads.uni-passau.de,
Gordon.Fraser@uni-passau.de

Abstract. The increasing popularity of mobile apps implies a need for automated test generation techniques for Android apps. Unlike other domains where automated test generation has been applied successfully, such as unit test generation, test execution for Android apps is computationally expensive: Tests are executed in an emulator, the app under test needs to be restarted after every test execution, and even individual actions within a test may take in the range of seconds to execute. This is inhibitive for approaches that rely on frequent execution of tests, such as search-based testing, which requires test executions to calculate fitness values. A common approach in evolutionary search is to use surrogate models as a means to reduce the costs of fitness calculation. In this paper, we introduce an approach to integrate surrogate models for testing Android apps: The surrogate model is an abstraction of the state-based behaviour of the graphical user interface, and can predict traces for already explored behaviour, thus avoiding costly test executions. We integrate this surrogate model in the search-based test generator MATE and perform an empirical study on a set of 10 Android apps. Results indicate that both the number of evaluated test cases and the resulting coverage can be increased significantly.

Keywords: Android · Surrogate model · Automated test generation

1 Introduction

The popularity of mobile apps causes a high demand for automated testing approaches. Most practical approaches for testing Android apps rely on running many tests, generated randomly or using model-based as well as search-based techniques [13]. In contrast to other common domains of automated test generation (e.g., unit test generation), the test execution process in Android is computationally very costly, as a single action may take several seconds to complete [12], and the necessary restarts of an app under test (AUT) between tests takes substantial time [9]. In addition, by construction random or search-based techniques will frequently produce very similar or redundant tests that exercise the identical behaviour. This affects the effectiveness of test generation.

M. Papadakis and S. R. Vergilio (Eds.): SSBSE 2022, LNCS 13711, pp. 51–66, 2022.
https://doi.org/10.1007/978-3-031-21251-2_4

In evolutionary computation, a common approach to overcome challenges caused by the high computational costs of fitness evaluations is to create *surrogate models* that can predict the outcome or fitness of some of the individuals of the search quicker than an actual evaluation would be [26]. However, this approach has not yet seen wide-spread use in search-based test generation, and is usually limited to cases where classical regression models can serve to predict fitness values [18]. Integrating the concept of surrogate models into the process of Android test generation requires models that can make state-based predictions.

State-based models (GUI models) are often used in Android testing to model the visible states of an app and the reactive behaviour in terms of transitions triggered by user events. In this paper, we extend these GUI models such that they predict execution traces for individual actions or entire tests. After repeatedly exploring similar behaviour, the surrogate model learns to predict most actions, thus saving the search budget for additional exploration and hence discovering yet uncovered behaviour and code.

We have implemented this approach as an extension of the MATE search-based test generator for Android [10], which supports state-of-the-art many objective test generation for Android driven by coverage-based fitness functions. Using our prototype implementation, we empirically study the influence of the chosen state abstraction, which determines the size and precision of the model. In detail, the main contributions of this paper are as follows:

- We introduce the concept of surrogate models in the context of search-based testing for Android.
- We provide a prototype implementation by extending the search-based test generator MATE.
- We empirically evaluate which abstraction level (fidelity level) of the surrogate model leads to the best trade off between achieved coverage and number of evaluated tests.
- We empirically evaluate how many restart operations can be avoided by using a surrogate model.
- We empirically evaluate the effects of the surrogate model on the coverage achieved by a state-of-the-art many objective search.

The results indicate that predicting actions with a surrogate model can be beneficial in terms of the number of evaluated tests, app restarts, and resulting activity and basic block coverage.

2   Background

The approach described in this paper combines (1) Search-based testing of Android apps, (2) surrogate models, and (3) Android GUI models.

2.1   Automated Android Testing

A basic approach to automatically test Android apps is to send random input actions. This approach has been shown to be effective, and often serves as a basis for further testing strategies [13], and is also applied as a form of fuzzing with the intent to find crashes, which may benefit from sending valid and invalid test data [13]. Search-based testing (e.g., [3,10,16,17]) extends random approaches by including (1) fitness functions that evaluate how close test executions are to reaching a testing objective (e.g., code coverage), and (2) search algorithms that make use of the fitness function to guide the generation and evolution of tests towards reaching the objective. Since deriving classical coverage-based fitness functions for Android apps is challenging, a recent trend lies in applying reinforcement learning techniques such as Q-Learning [25], SARSA [22], or Deep Learning [21], which aim to learn how to explore apps. Android test generators are often complemented with finite state machine (FSM) models, where states may describe activities or GUI states, and edges refer to actions that trigger the respective transition from one state to another. In this paper, we use this type of models to build surrogate models.

2.2 Surrogate Models

A surrogate model is used to mimic the response of some original model with the benefit of being computationally cheaper. Common surrogate models such as polynomial response surface (PRS), radial basis functions (RBF), kriging, artificial neural networks (ANNs) and support vector machines (SVMs) [20,24] use a specific level of fidelity, i.e., level of abstraction. Low fidelity models are computationally cheaper, but less accurate. In contrast, high fidelity models are preciser but also more expensive. Since the level of fidelity has an important impact on the surrogate model, prior research has also investigated multi-fidelity models that combine low and high fidelity models, hybrid models that combine multiple different single-fidelity models and adaptive sampling strategies that try to improve the accuracy by so-called infilling strategies [24].

In the domain of evolutionary algorithms surrogate models are used to lower the cost of fitness function evaluations [26]. Typically the surrogate model learns from a training set, which can be either constructed through sampling strategies or candidate solutions obtained from running the evolutionary algorithm without the surrogate model [26]. While surrogate models are common in many domains of evolutionary computation, they have only rarely been used in the scope of search-based testing so far. For example, Matinnejad et al. [18] used classical regression models to predict fitness values when testing Simulink models. In contrast, the application context of Android apps requires surrogate models to make predictions about state-based behaviour.

2.3 Android GUI Models

An Android app is composed of four different types of components, whereas activities enable the graphical interaction from the user perspective. Such an activity consists of multiple widgets arranged in a hierarchical structure, where most of those widgets enable some sort of interaction, e.g., clicking on a button. This in turn triggers some action, e.g., opening another activity.

One can form a GUI model for an Android app by considering those inter-actions as edges in a finite state machine (FSM), while the states are typically represented through abstractions of the physical screen state [6], e.g., the widget hierarchy. A more abstract representation of a GUI model is an Activity Transition Graph (ATG) as outlined in [5], where the states refer to the activities and the edges represent activity transitions.

Baek et al. [6] categorise different state equivalence definitions from a low (fine-grained model) to high degree of abstraction (coarse-grained model):

Package Name Two GUI states are equal if they refer to the same AUT. This essentially means that the AUT is represented by a single abstract state, but further states may represent other apps or the home screen.

Activity Name Two GUI states are equal if they refer to the same activity.

Widget Composition Two GUI states are equal if the widgets in the UI hierarchy are the same in terms of type, e.g., Button, and position.

Widget Composition + Event Handlers Two GUI states are considered equal if the widgets in the UI hierarchy are the same in terms of type (e.g., button), and position as well as share the same event handlers.

Widget Content Two GUI states are equal if the widgets in the UI hierarchy are the same in terms of type (e.g., button), and position as well as share the same text and content description attributes.

Prior research suggests that stricter state equivalences may lead to worse results than focusing on the structure of GUI elements [14]. An orthogonal app-roach to achieve this lies in using distance metrics such as cosine similarity [15], Jaccard similarity [12], or Hamming distance [12] on vectors derived from GUI state information to determine the similarity of two states when deciding on equivalence, rather than exact matches of state information.

3   Android Testing with Surrogate Models

In order to explore the use of surrogate models in Android testing, we extend the search-based test generator MATE with a surrogate model that is a state-machine based on equivalence of GUI states. The search algorithms themselves do not require adaptation, but the point of integration is the test execution, which is underlying the fitness calculation.

3.1   Search-Based Android Testing: MATE

In order to explore the concept of surrogate models, we use the open source search-based test generator MATE, which was originally designed for automated accessibility testing [10]. Later on it was enhanced with a rich set of evolutionary search algorithms [23], making it an ideal vehicle for our experiments. An indi-vidual or chromosome in the genetic algorithm is typically represented by a test case in MATE and each such test case is composed of a list of actions. MATE supports both single- and multi-objective algorithms and the available fitness functions range from coverage metrics to approach level and branch distance.

MATE consists of two components, *MATE-Client* and *MATE-Server*. The client is composed of two APKs that run on the emulator alongside with the AUT. In contrast, the server is run on a local machine and performs resource-intensive tasks, e.g., computing the control flow graph (which may be of substantial size in the inter-procedural case). MATE supports both UI and system events and can report activity, method, branch and basic block coverage. It leverages the UiAutomator API [2] to locate widgets on the screen and makes use of ADB [1] to obtain information about the device and AUT state. MATE supports apps targeting an API level between 19 and 28.

3.2 Surrogate Model for Android GUIs

The surrogate model can be viewed as a directed graph $G = (V, E)$ where a state $s \in V$ describes an abstraction of a physical screen state. Depending on the chosen state equivalence level, a state might refer to an activity or to a precise abstraction of the DOM tree. Out of the state equivalence levels described in Sect. 2.3 we employ the following in our implementation:

Activity Name Two states are equal if they refer to the same activity.
Widget Composition Two states are equal if the UI hierarchy composed of widgets is identical. This means that the widgets are of the same type, e.g., Button, and share the same coordinates.
Widget Content Two states are equal if not only the UI hierarchy matches in terms of type and coordinates but also the widgets' text and content description attributes are identical.

A too coarse-grained state equivalence level like the package name may limit a thorough exploration, as the AUT model would often be represented by a single state, which is why we excluded this state equivalence level. The chosen levels are a trade-off between a too coarse and a too fine-grained model, establish a baseline for future comparison, and we thus leave investigations of even finer-grained levels such as *Widget Composition + Event Handlers* or the use of distance metrics such as *Cosine similarity* for future work.

An edge $e \in E$ is a tuple $(s_i, a_i, s_j, t_i, c_k)$, which represents a transition from a source state $s_i \in V$ to a target state $s_j \in V$ with an action $a_i \in A$, a set of partial traces t_i and a transition counter c_k. An action a_i is composed of an action type, e.g., click, and additional parameters like the underlying widget or the input for text fields, while the traces t_i represent a set of covered targets, e.g., basic blocks. By traversing the path described through the actions of the test case, one can fully re-assemble the full trace of the entire test case. These traces are relevant for the fitness evaluation where one needs to decide whether a certain target, e.g., basic block, is covered or not. The last component of the edge tuple maintains how often the given transition was taken so far. Every time we execute an action the respective transition counter is increased.

3.3   Test Execution with a Surrogate Model

The overall objective of a surrogate model is to allow calculating fitness values without actual test executions, thus leading to a more effective use of the search budget, as test executions and the restart operations they necessity are costly. Our surrogate model supports this process by predicting the outcome of individual actions in a test in terms of the resulting state as well as the resulting traces. That is, the surrogate model attempts to construct an execution trace without actual execution, which can then serve as input to the fitness function. The initial model by construction cannot predict any actions, but after a certain number of iterations, we expect the model to improve such that it can predict the outcome, i.e., the target state and the traces, of more and more actions. Depending on the chosen state equivalence level and hence the granularity of the model this trend towards predicting more actions is reached earlier or later.

An overview of integrating the surrogate model into the test execution process is illustrated in Fig. 1: A search algorithm provides test cases in the form of sequences of actions $T = \langle a_1, \ldots, a_n \rangle$, $a_i \in A$, and produces a resulting list of states $S = \langle s_1, \ldots s_n \rangle$ as well as an execution trace represented as a list of partial traces $E = \langle t_1, \ldots t_n \rangle$. Given a test case to be executed, we initialise S and E as empty lists. A test case T is executed by iterating over the actions of T. For each action a_i the surrogate model is queried to determine whether the outcome of a_i can be predicted or not. The outcome of an action a can be predicted in state s if there exists an outgoing transition from state s to some other state t labelled with action a in the surrogate model. If such a transition exists, the resulting state and partial trace are appended to S and E, respectively. In addition, the surrogate model keeps track of all predicted actions in a list of cached actions C. This list stores all actions that are not executed immediately but may need to be executed if the model cannot predict the complete test case. The execution on the surrogate model further keeps track of the new current state.

If the outcome of the selected action cannot be predicted in the current state, the AUT needs to be set to the correct state by executing the list of cached actions C; then the new action a_i is executed. The surrogate model is then updated with a new transition from s to the observed resulting state, with a transition labelled with the selected action and the traces produced by the action. In addition, the associated transition counter is increased and the list of cached actions C is cleared, since the app is now in a known state.

This process continues until the last action a_n of T has been executed, or we leave the AUT through a crash or regular transition. Once the test case is completely predicted or executed, we perform some final tasks like re-assembling the correct action sequence from the cached and executed actions as well as aggregating the traces from the individual actions for fitness evaluation. Lastly, the AUT has to be restarted to ensure that the next test case starts in a clean state if any of the actions had to be executed on the actual app. If the surrogate model was able to predict all actions successfully, no restart is necessary.

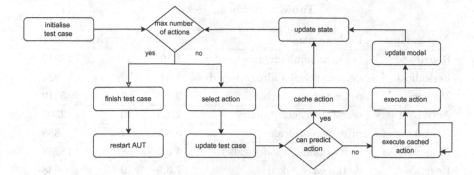

Fig. 1. Overview of integrating the surrogate model in the test execution process. A test case is iteratively filled with actions until the maximal number of actions is reached or the AUT is left. During updating the test case with a new action, the surrogate model is consulted whether the outcome of the action can be predicted or not.

During the test execution one may encounter the following issues:

Leaving the AUT: If the execution of a cached action leaves the AUT, e.g., causes a crash, we finish the test case at this point as we would do in the regular case.

Non-applicable actions: If we need to execute a sequence of cached actions, we may land in an unexpected state that does not match what the surrogate model expects such that the follow-up action might be not applicable anymore. In this case we pick a random applicable action and proceed.

Non-deterministic actions: There might be multiple outgoing transitions from the current state with a selected action. In such a case, we pick the transition that was taken most often, based on the transition counter.

Thus overall, the precision of the surrogate model depends on (1) the chosen state equivalence level and (2) the deterministic behaviour of the AUT.

4   Evaluation

We aim to answer the following research questions:

- **RQ1:** Does the state equivalence level influence the effectivness of the surrogate model in terms of number of test cases and coverage?
- **RQ2:** Can the surrogate model avoid costly restart operations?
- **RQ3:** Does the use of the surrogate model increase the number of test cases and coverage?

4.1   Experimental Setup

For the empirical evaluation, we use the ten study subjects presented in Table 1, which originate from a prior study [23]. The MATE testing framework has

Table 1. Study subjects.

App name	Package name	Version	Activities	Blocks
RedReader	org.quantumbadger.redreader	1.16	20	17817
Periodical	de.arnowelzel.android.periodical	1.64	8	924
Markor	net.gsantner.markor	2.5.0	6	5519
Activity Diary	de.rampro.activitydiary	1.4.0	10	2307
Rental Calc	protect.rentalcalc	0.5.1	12	858
MoneyWallet	com.oriondev.moneywallet	4.0.5.9	38	18258
Easy xkcd	de.tap.easy_xkcd	7.3.9	9	4638
TSCH_BYL	de.drhoffmannsoftware	1.16–11	9	618
Shopping List	com.woefe.shoppinglist	0.11.0	4	845
Bierverkostung	de.retujo.bierverkostung	1.2.1	13	4333

been configured to explore each app with the *MIO* algorithm [4] for 3 h, where we used F = 0.5, Pr = 0.5, n = 10 and m = 10 as outlined in the original paper. The testing targets for each app represent the basic blocks and the fitness function for each target evaluates whether the basic block was covered or not. The maximal number of actions per test case have been set to 50. To compensate for randomness, we repeated the runs twelve times per app and configuration. This leads to a total execution time of roughly 360 h.

We conducted the experiments on a compute cluster, where each node features two Intel Xeon E5-2620v4 CPUs (16 cores) with 2.10 GHz and 256 GB of RAM, and runs Debian GNU/Linux 11 with Java 11. We limit each execution of MATE to ten cores and 32 GB of RAM, where 16 GB of RAM are reserved for the emulator. The emulator (Nexus 5) employs a x86 image running API level 25 (Android 7.1.1).

The implementation is open source and available at https://github.com/mate-android-testing (experiments in this paper were conducted using Git tag SSBSE22).

4.2 Experiments

To address the research questions, we defined four configurations *C1* to *C4*. *C1* refers to the configuration where we did not use a surrogate model, while *C2* to *C4* represents the configurations with the different state equivalence levels (*Activity Name, Widget Composition, Widget Content*).

In order to answer **RQ1**, we compare the configurations *C2* to *C4* in terms of number of test cases evaluated (i.e., predicted or actually executed) and coverage (activity and basic block coverage), where both objectives are assumed to be maximised. We use tournament ranking to determine which configuration is the best one: For each pairwise comparison of configurations and apps a configuration gets a point if there is a statistic significance ($\alpha = 0.05$) using the *Mann-Whitney-U-Test* and if the *Vargha-Delaney* effect size reports a value greater than 0.5.

Table 2. Comparing the different surrogate model configurations regarding the average number of evaluated tests and coverage.

App	C2			C3			C4		
	Tests	AC	BC	Tests	AC	BC	Tests	AC	BC
org.quantumbadger.redreader	2311.75	28.75	37.35	233.00	53.33	53.02	231.92	52.50	53.52
de.arnowelzel.android.periodical	3441.08	65.62	65.91	699.92	86.46	78.07	520.08	87.50	79.27
net.gsantner.markor	3236.42	30.95	20.64	1302.25	60.71	47.58	1231.42	60.71	46.00
de.rampro.activitydiary	1467.50	70.45	61.56	353.75	82.58	69.85	283.92	83.33	69.26
protect.rentalcalc	4725.33	43.06	32.19	1143.75	63.19	49.70	1143.75	65.97	52.67
com.oriondev.moneywallet	2685.92	12.28	7.76	1228.08	28.51	16.30	1013.50	27.85	15.83
de.tap.easy_xkcd	2014.58	28.79	27.95	372.08	57.58	49.04	574.33	59.09	48.70
de.drhoffmannsoftware	4062.67	96.30	26.36	708.42	100.00	33.78	895.83	100.00	32.78
com.woefe.shoppinglist	3164.08	37.50	47.61	1088.75	100.00	77.95	1226.92	100.00	76.03
de.retujo.bierverkostung	2117.42	51.92	28.94	525.58	73.08	38.21	634.92	76.28	39.04
Average	2922.68	46.56	35.63	765.56	70.54	51.35	775.66	71.32	51.41

To address **RQ2**, we track the number of avoided and total restarts for the configurations C2 to C4. Regarding **RQ3**, we solely need to compare the best configuration obtained from evaluating the first research question to configuration C1. To make a statistical statement, we report in addition to the number of evaluated tests and coverage the p-values.

4.3 RQ1: State Equivalence Levels

Table 2 shows the resulting number of test cases, activity (AC) and basic block coverage (BC) for the three different surrogate model configurations C2 to C4. The configuration C2 clearly outperforms the other two configurations in terms of evaluated test cases, but apparently remains behind when considering both coverage criteria. The configurations C3 and C4 behave quite similarly throughout all three criteria.

The tournament ranking illustrated in Table 3 confirms this interpretation. C2 outperforms the remaining configurations in terms of evaluated test cases: it is significantly better in eight cases. However, the lower precision in state matching comes at the price of lower coverage: The configuration C4 is slightly better than C3 when looking at activity and basic block coverage. Both C3 and C4 are never better than C2 respective to the number of evaluated test cases.

Summary (RQ1): Using a coarse-grained state equivalence level like the activity name (C2) enables the generation of many test cases but at the cost of significantly less coverage. Since we favour coverage over the number of evaluated test cases, a trade-off is configuration C4 as it evaluates slightly more test cases than C3 while achieving the best coverage results on average.

4.4 RQ2: Effects on App Restarts

Table 4 reports the number of actually executed restarts, number of evaluated tests, and the percentage of restarts saved for the configurations C2 to C4. The

Table 3. Tournament ranking of surrogate model configurations, counting statistically significant differences on all pairwise comparisons of configurations.

Criteria	C2	C3	C4
AC	0	8	9
BC	0	10	10
Tests	20	0	0

Table 4. Comparison of the average number of restarts, evaluated tests and the percentage of saved restarts for different surrogate model configurations.

App	C2			C3			C4		
	Restarts	Tests	% saved	Restarts	Tests	% saved	Restarts	Tests	% saved
org.quantumbadger.redreader	37.50	2311.75	98.38	144.00	233.00	38.40	140.08	231.92	39.82
de.arnowelzel.android.periodical	43.33	3441.08	98.74	213.50	699.92	69.52	219.83	520.08	57.81
net.gsantner.markor	7.75	3236.42	99.76	160.00	1302.25	87.72	148.58	1231.42	87.94
de.rampro.activitydiary	146.67	1467.50	90.01	205.00	353.75	42.20	209.75	283.92	26.34
protect.rentalcalc	52.25	4725.33	98.89	240.33	1143.75	79.00	239.50	1143.75	79.08
com.oriondev.moneywallet	24.42	2685.92	99.09	196.83	1228.08	83.98	206.00	1013.50	79.69
de.tap.easy_xkcd	58.33	2014.58	97.10	225.08	372.08	39.66	194.75	574.33	66.13
de.drhoffmannsoftware	75.58	4062.67	98.14	266.17	708.42	62.47	243.58	895.83	72.83
com.woefe.shoppinglist	6.67	3164.08	99.79	247.25	1088.75	77.30	224.83	1226.92	81.68
de.retujo.bierverkostung	137.42	2117.42	93.51	240.42	525.58	54.31	230.25	634.92	63.77
Average	58.99	2922.68	97.98	213.86	765.56	72.09	205.72	775.66	73.50

less fine-grained the surrogate model, the more actions and finally tests can be predicted, directly leading to a higher number of saved restarts. Recall that all actions of a test case need to be predicted in order to save the restart operation. Configuration *C2* confirms this trend, but also the configurations *C3* and *C4* having a more moderate number of total restarts can benefit extremely from the surrogate model. More than 70% of the restarts can be avoided in both cases. The time saved by avoiding these restarts is available for the search algorithm to explore more diverse test cases.

Summary (*RQ2*): Using a more coarse-grained state equivalence level leads to the prediction of more actions and entire test cases, but even the more fine-grained models can avoid more than 70% of the restarts.

4.5   RQ3: Effects on Tests and Coverage

Table 5 shows that configuration *C4* evaluates more than twice the number of tests than the configuration without the surrogate model (775 vs. 342). We can note a statistical difference in eight out of ten apps in favour of *C4*.

To understand whether this increase in the number of tests as well as the reduction in necessary app restarts has an impact on coverage, Table 6 summarizes the results in terms of activity coverage and basic block coverage achieved with (C4) and without surrogate model (C1). For the *de.arnowelzel.*

Table 5. Comparing *C1* to *C4* in terms of average number of evaluated tests.

App	Tests			
	C1	C4	p	$\hat{A}_{12}$
org.quantumbadger.redreader	280.08	231.92	0.08	0.72
de.arnowelzel.android.periodical	314.67	520.08	<0.001	0.10
net.gsantner.markor	321.83	1231.42	<0.001	0.00
de.rampro.activitydiary	318.33	283.92	0.30	0.63
protect.rentalcalc	399.92	1143.75	<0.001	0.08
com.oriondev.moneywallet	430.08	1013.50	<0.001	0.01
de.tap.easy_xkcd	273.92	574.33	<0.001	0.14
de.drhoffmannsoftware	324.92	895.83	<0.001	0.08
com.woefe.shoppinglist	410.67	1226.92	<0.001	0.00
de.retujo.bierverkostung	345.75	634.92	0.02	0.22
Average	342.02	775.66	–	–

android.periodical, *net.gsantner.markor*, and *com.oriondev.moneywallet* apps the surrogate model leads to significantly higher activity coverage. For basic block coverage the surrogate model leads to significantly better results for *de.arnowelzel.android.periodical*, *net.gsantner.markor*, and *de.retujo.bierverkostung*. For *de.tap.easy_xkcd* the activity coverage achieved with the surrogate model is significantly lower, although there is no significant difference in basic block coverage. For *de.drhoffmannsoftware* and *com.woefe.shoppinglist* both configurations achieve 100% activity coverage.

Considering *de.tap.easy_xkcd*, the lower activity coverage can be explained by the use of a progress bar widget in the app: The surrogate model treats different values of the progress bar as different states. We conjecture that the largest improvements in coverage are caused when there are fewer widgets in the activities, such that the surrogate model can effectively predict the outcome and help the surrogate model explore new widgets. In those cases where there is no significant difference, it appears that the search was unable to make use of the additional tests. This is likely influenced by the inadequate guidance provided by the fitness functions: Since the fitness function only provides binary information on whether a coverage goal was reached, the search may not have sufficient incentive to drive the exploration towards more relevant parts of the search space. We conjecture that the effects of the surrogate model will be larger if future work succeeds in improving the fitness landscape for Android test generation.

Summary (*RQ3*): The configuration using the surrogate model clearly evaluates more tests than the configuration without. The surrogate model increases activity and basic block coverage on average.

Table 6. Comparing *C1* to *C4* in terms of average activity and basic block coverage.

App	AC				BC			
	C1	C4	p	$\hat{A}_{12}$	C1	C4	p	$\hat{A}_{12}$
org.quantumbadger.redreader	54.17	52.50	0.49	0.58	53.02	53.52	0.37	0.39
de.arnowelzel.android.periodical	81.25	87.50	0.02	0.29	72.60	79.27	<0.001	0.01
net.gsantner.markor	54.76	60.71	0.03	0.31	37.83	46.99	<0.001	0.03
de.rampro.activitydiary	82.58	83.33	0.79	0.47	69.21	69.26	0.98	0.51
protect.rentalcalc	60.42	65.97	0.46	0.41	47.53	52.67	0.47	0.41
com.oriondev.moneywallet	25.22	27.85	0.04	0.26	14.88	15.83	0.16	0.33
de.tap.easy_xkcd	65.91	59.09	0.02	0.76	48.36	48.70	0.84	0.53
de.drhoffmannsoftware	100.00	100.00	–	0.50	29.90	32.78	0.09	0.30
com.woefe.shoppinglist	100.00	100.00	–	0.50	78.05	76.03	0.44	0.60
de.retujo.bierverkostung	75.00	76.28	0.51	0.43	36.90	39.04	0.05	0.26
Average	69.93	71.32	–	–	48.83	51.41	–	–

5   Related Work

In this section we review state equivalence levels found in the literature and summarize where surrogate models have been used for automated testing.

5.1   State Equivalence

The effectiveness of a state-based surrogate model depends on the chosen level of state abstraction. Baek et al. [6] proposed five different GUI comparison criteria (GUICC) that range from considering only the package name to inspecting the content of widgets. In comparison to our work, we utilize three very similar state equivalence definitions. The activity name GUICC is a 1:1 match, while the second and third state equivalence level proposed in Sect. 2.3 also compare one time the structure and the other time the content of the widgets. We excluded the package name GUICC because we believe it is too abstract (one state for the entire AUT) and thus is likely to produce low coverage results. The configuration *C2* using the activity name essentially confirms these concerns. Prior work [6] indicates that a lower level of abstraction (more fine-grained GUICC) leads to a higher coverage. We can conclude the same findings as the Table 2 shows.

A^{3}E [5] utilizes a static and dynamic activity transition graph to represent the GUI model, where the states are represented through the activities of the AUT. This would only allow a comparison based on the activity name, but we are also interested in comparing the individual widgets on the screen. Thus, we stick to a more fine-grained GUI model using screens as states.

The empirical study by Jiang et al. [12] evaluates which factors impact the effectiveness and efficiency of Android test generators. Apart from considering different state traversal techniques and waiting times between two inputs, five different state equivalence metrics are examined. This includes, among others,

Cosine and *Jaccard similarity* as well as *Hamming distance*. Also here, a more fine-grained comparison is likely to achieve a higher coverage. We did not include similarity or distance metrics, but focused on producing a baseline.

Lee et al. [14] discuss different state equivalence checks, including a content hash over all widgets, a structure hash over the ui hierarchy and a heuristic that considers the event handlers in case of similar lists. The first two metrics are similar to the state equivalence levels we proposed, i.e. comparing the structure and content of the widgets. The idea of looking at the event handlers in case of list widgets is definitely a valid point for future research.

DECAF [15] extracts feature vectors for states consisting of a concatenation of multiple widget attributes. If the *Cosine similarity* is above a pre-defined threshold, two states are considered identical. We plan to extend our experiments to include such similarity metrics in the future.

5.2   Surrogate Models in Automated Testing

Surrogate models have recently been integrated into test generation algorithms for different types of search approaches. Matinnejad et al. [18] introduced surrogate models in the context of Model-in-the-Loop testing for continous controllers. The meta-heuristic search algorithm uses a combination of dimensionality reduction and a surrogate model in order to scale the testing for large, multidimensional input spaces. In particular, the surrogate model enables predicting the outcome of a fitness function in a fast manner. Abdessalem et al. [8] evaluate a testing approach for Advanced Driver Assistance Systems (ADAS) based on a combination of multi-objective search and surrogate models. The neural network based surrogate model enables a faster exploration of the input search space within a limited time budget. Haq et al. [11] extended many-objective search using a surrogate model in order to reduce the cost of simulations in the context of Automated Driving Systems. Their experiments on various types of classical surrogate models suggest that the surrogate model leads to a more effective and efficient detection of safety violations, similar to how our surrogate model improves testing. Similarly, Beglerovic et al. [7] use the classical approach of Kriging surrogate model for testing autonomous vehicles. Menghi et al. [19] apply numerical approximations of Cyber-Physical system (CPS) models as surrogate model to improve testing. Initially, a surrogate model is trained by sample input and outputs of the CPS under test. If the surrogate model produces a failure-revealing test, the test is checked against the original model. If there is a mismatch, the surrogate model is refined. Otherwise, the test represents a valid failure. The main differences of our work in contrast to these approaches are that we use a state-based model suitable for GUI exploration, and use this surrogate model to predict the outcomes of actions and only indirectly for the evaluation of the fitness function. Furthermore, the integration of our model requires no adaptations of the search algorithms.

6   Conclusions

Search-based testing involves the execution of many potentially very similar action sequences. In the domain of Android testing, the costs for the test execution are high, as individual actions as well as restarts of the AUT inbetween test executions take time. To overcome this problem, we proposed in this paper the integration of a surrogate model in the test execution process. The model aims to predict individual actions or, in the best case, entire tests. If a test case can be predicted, fitness calculation can be performed on the predicted execution trace, without actual execution. We integrated this approach into the test generator MATE and evaluated the effectiveness of the surrogate model in terms of the number of tests and coverage on a set of ten open source apps. In particular, we considered three different state equivalence levels that directly influence the granularity of the surrogate model. The results indicate that a coarse-grained model can evaluate substantially more tests but may inhibit coverage. In contrast, selecting a more fine-grained model leads to a moderate increase in the number of evaluated tests while achieving reasonable coverage values. Independently from the chosen state equivalence level, the test execution can avoid a large number of costly restart operations. Overall, search-based testing can benefit from a surrogate model in terms of evaluated tests, number of necessary restarts, and resulting coverage.

For future work we plan to evaluate the influence of using a different strategy for non-deterministic actions. Instead of picking the transition with the highest visit counter, we could introduce a threshold that must be exceeded such that we can predict the outcome of the given action. Alternatively, we could choose the transition that includes the largest number of traces. Another option for future work is the evaluation of further state equivalence levels as well as distance metrics. For instance, one could consider additional attributes like the visibility of the widgets in the state comparison. Last but not least, we would like to replicate the study on a larger set of subjects.

References

1. Android debug bridge (ADB). https://developer.android.com/studio/command-line/adb. Accessed 21 June 2022
2. Write automated tests with UI automator. https://developer.android.com/training/testing/other-components/ui-automator. Accessed 21 June 2022
3. Amalfitano, D., Amatucci, N., Fasolino, A.R., Tramontana, P.: AGRippin: a novel search based testing technique for android applications. In: Proceedings of the 3rd International Workshop on Software Development Lifecycle for Mobile, DeMobile 2015, pp. 5–12. ACM (2015)
4. Arcuri, A.: Many independent objective (MIO) algorithm for test suite generation. In: Menzies, T., Petke, J. (eds.) SSBSE 2017. LNCS, vol. 10452, pp. 3–17. Springer, Cham (2017). https://doi.org/10.1007/978-3-319-66299-2_1
5. Azim, T., Neamtiu, I.: Targeted and depth-first exploration for systematic testing of android apps. SIGPLAN Not. **48**(10), 641–660 (2013)

6. Baek, Y.M., Bae, D.H.: Automated model-based android GUI testing using multi-level GUI comparison criteria. In: Proceedings of the 31st IEEE/ACM International Conference on Automated Software Engineering, pp. 238–249. ACM (2016)
7. Beglerovic, H., Stolz, M., Horn, M.: Testing of autonomous vehicles using surrogate models and stochastic optimization. In: 2017 IEEE 20th International Conference on Intelligent Transportation Systems (ITSC), pp. 1–6 (2017)
8. Ben Abdessalem, R., Nejati, S., Briand, L.C., Stifter, T.: Testing advanced driver assistance systems using multi-objective search and neural networks. In: 31st IEEE/ACM International Conference on Automated Software Engineering (ASE), pp. 63–74 (2016)
9. Choi, W., Necula, G., Sen, K.: Guided GUI testing of android apps with minimal restart and approximate learning. SIGPLAN Not. **48**(10), 623–640 (2013)
10. Eler, M.M., Rojas, J.M., Ge, Y., Fraser, G.: Automated accessibility testing of mobile apps. In: ICST, pp. 116–126. IEEE Computer Society (2018)
11. Haq, F.U., Shin, D., Briand, L.: Efficient online testing for DNN-enabled systems using surrogate-assisted and many-objective optimization. In: 2022 IEEE/ACM 44th International Conference on Software Engineering (ICSE), pp. 811–822 (2022)
12. Jiang, B., Zhang, Y., Chan, W.K., Zhang, Z.: A systematic study on factors impacting GUI traversal-based test case generation techniques for android applications. IEEE Trans. Reliab. **68**(3), 913–926 (2019)
13. Kong, P., Li, L., Gao, J., Liu, K., Bissyandé, T.F., Klein, J.: Automated testing of android apps: a systematic literature review. IEEE Trans. Reliab. **68**(1), 45–66 (2019)
14. Lee, K., Flinn, J., Giuli, T., Noble, B., Peplin, C.: AMC: verifying user interface properties for vehicular applications. In: Proceeding of the 11th Annual International Conference on Mobile Systems, Applications, and Services, MobiSys 2013, pp. 1–12. Association for Computing Machinery, New York (2013)
15. Liu, B., Nath, S., Govindan, R., Liu, J.: DECAF: detecting and characterizing ad fraud in mobile apps. In: 11th USENIX Symposium on Networked Systems Design and Implementation (NSDI 14), pp. 57–70. USENIX Association (2014)
16. Mahmood, R., Mirzaei, N., Malek, S.: EvoDroid: segmented evolutionary testing of android apps. In: Proceedings of the 22nd ACM SIGSOFT International Symposium on Foundations of Software Engineering, FSE 2014, pp. 599–609. ACM (2014)
17. Mao, K., Harman, M., Jia, Y.: Sapienz: multi-objective automated testing for android applications. In: Proceedings of the 25th International Symposium on Software Testing and Analysis, ISSTA 2016, pp. 94–105. ACM (2016)
18. Matinnejad, R., Nejati, S., Briand, L., Brcukmann, T.: Mil testing of highly configurable continuous controllers: scalable search using surrogate models. In: Proceedings of the 29th ACM/IEEE International Conference on Automated Software Engineering, pp. 163–174 (2014)
19. Menghi, C., Nejati, S., Briand, L., Parache, Y.I.: Approximation-refinement testing of compute-intensive cyber-physical models: An approach based on system identification. In: Proceedings of the ACM/IEEE 42nd International Conference on Software Engineering, ICSE 2020, pp. 372–384. ACM (2020)
20. Razavi, S., Tolson, B.A., Burn, D.H.: Review of surrogate modeling in water resources. Water Resour. Res. **48**(7) (2012)
21. Romdhana, A., Merlo, A., Ceccato, M., Tonella, P.: Deep reinforcement learning for black-box testing of android apps. ACM Trans. Softw. Eng. Methodol. (2022)
22. Rummery, G., Niranjan, M.: On-line Q-learning using connectionist systems. Technical report CUED/F-INFENG/TR 166 (1994)

23. Sell, L., Auer, M., Frädrich, C., Gruber, M., Werli, P., Fraser, G.: An empirical evaluation of search algorithms for app testing. In: Gaston, C., Kosmatov, N., Le Gall, P. (eds.) ICTSS 2019. LNCS, vol. 11812, pp. 123–139. Springer, Cham (2019). https://doi.org/10.1007/978-3-030-31280-0_8
24. Song, X., Lv, L., Sun, W.: A radial basis function-based multi-fidelity surrogate model: exploring correlation between high-fidelity and low-fidelity models. Struct. Multidisc. Optim. **60**, 965–981 (2019)
25. Sutton, R.S., Barto, A.G.: Reinforcement Learning: An Introduction. A Bradford Book, Cambridge (2018)
26. Tong, H., Huang, C., Minku, L.L., Yao, X.: Surrogate models in evolutionary single-objective optimization: a new taxonomy and experimental study. Inf. Sci. **562**, 414–437 (2021)

Guess What: Test Case Generation for Javascript with Unsupervised Probabilistic Type Inference

Dimitri Stallenberg, Mitchell Olsthoorn[(✉)] [iD], and Annibale Panichella [iD]

Delft University of Technology, Delft, The Netherlands
D.M.Stallenberg@student.tudelft.nl,
{M.J.G.Olsthoorn,A.Panichella}@tudelft.nl

Abstract. Search-based test case generation approaches make use of static type information to determine which data types should be used for the creation of new test cases. Dynamically typed languages like JavaScript, however, do not have this type information. In this paper, we propose an unsupervised probabilistic type inference approach to infer data types within the test case generation process. We evaluated the proposed approach on a benchmark of 98 units under test (*i.e.,* exported classes and functions) compared to random type sampling *w.r.t.* branch coverage. Our results show that our type inference approach achieves a statistically significant increase in 56% of the test files with up to 71% of branch coverage compared to the baseline.

Keywords: Empirical software engineering · Search-based software testing · Test case generation · Javascript · Type inference

1 Introduction

Over the last few decades, researchers have developed various techniques for automating test case generation [31]. In particular, search-based approaches have been shown to (1) achieve higher code coverage [25] and (2) have fewer smells [37] compared to manually-written test cases, and (3) detect unknown bugs [1,2,21]. Furthermore, generated tests significantly reduce the time needed for testing and debugging [42], and have been successfully used in industry (*e.g.,* [3,11,30]).

These approaches make use of static type information to (1) generate primitives and objects to pass to constructors and function calls, and (2) determine which branch distance function to use. Without this type information, the test case generation process has to randomly guess which types are compatible with the parameter specification of the constructor or function call and would not have guidance to solve the binary flag problem. This greatly increases the search space and, therefore, makes the overall process less effective and efficient. Consequently, most of the work in this research area has focused on statically-typed programming languages like Java (*e.g.,* EVOSUITE [18]) and C (*e.g.,* AUSTIN [26]).

© The Author(s), under exclusive license to Springer Nature Switzerland AG 2022
M. Papadakis and S. R. Vergilio (Eds.): SSBSE 2022, LNCS 13711, pp. 67–82, 2022.
https://doi.org/10.1007/978-3-031-21251-2_5

Dynamically-typed programming languages introduce new challenges for unit-level test case generation. As reported by Lukasczyk *et al.* [28], state-of-the-art approaches used for statically-typed languages do not perform well on Python programs when type information is not available. According to the survey from Stack Overflow[1], Python and JavaScript are the two most commonly-used programming languages. Both languages are dynamically-typed, strengthening the importance of addressing these open challenges with the goal of increasing the adoption of test case generation tools in general.

In this paper, we focus on test case generation for JavaScript as, to the best of our knowledge, this is a research gap in the literature. In building our research, we build on top of the reported experience by Lukasczyk *et al.* [29] for Python programs. They addressed the input type challenge by incorporating Type4Py [32]—a deep neural network (DNN)—into the search process.

We propose a novel approach that incorporates unsupervised probabilistic type inference into the search-based test case generation process to infer the type information needed. An unsupervised type inference approach has two benefits compared to a DNN: (1) it does not require a labeled dataset with extensive training time, and (2) the model is explainable (*i.e.*, the decision can be traced back to a rule set). We build a prototype tool which implements the state-of-the-art many-objective search algorithm, DYNAMOSA, and the probabilistic type inference model for JavaScript. We investigate two different strategies for incorporating the probabilistic model into the main loop of DYNAMOSA, namely *proportional sampling* and *ranking*.

To evaluate the performance of the proposed approach, we performed an empirical study that investigates the baseline performance of our prototype (*i.e.*, using random type sampling) and the impact of the unsupervised probabilistic type inference *w.r.t.* branch coverage. To this aim, we constructed a benchmark consisting of 98 Units under Test (*i.e.*, exported classes and functions) of five popular open-source JavaScript projects, namely `Commander.js`, `Express`, `Moment.js`, `Javascript Algorithms`, and `Lodash`.

Our results show that integrating unsupervised probabilistic type inference improves branch coverage compared to random type sampling. Both the *ranking* and *proportional sampling* strategies significantly increase the number of branches covered by our approach (+9.3% and +12.6%, respectively). Out of the two strategies, *proportional sampling* outperforms *ranking* in 20 cases and loses in 4. In summary, we make the following contributions:

1. An unsupervised probabilistic type inference approach for search-based unit-level test case generation of JavaScript programs.
2. A prototype tool for automatically generating JavaScript unit-level test cases that incorporates this approach.[2]
3. A Benchmark consisting of 98 units under test from five popular open-source JavaScript projects.
4. A full replication package containing the results and the analysis scripts [43].

---

[1] https://survey.stackoverflow.co/2022/#most-popular-technologies-language.

[2] https://github.com/syntest-framework/syntest-javascript.

2   Background and Related Work

This section explains the background concepts and discusses the related work.

Test Case Generation. Writing test cases is an expensive, tedious, yet necessary activity for software quality assurance. Hence, researchers have proposed various techniques to semi-automate this process since the 1970s [15]. These techniques include symbolic execution [10], random testing [14], and meta-heuristics [31] (e.g., genetic algorithms). The latter category is often referred to as search-based software testing (SBST). SBST techniques have been successfully used in the literature to automate the creation of test cases for different testing levels [31], such as unit [19], integration [17], and system-level testing [6]. At unit-level, SBST techniques aim to generate test cases that optimize various test adequacy criteria, such as e.g., structural coverage and mutation score. Many different meta-heuristic search algorithms have been proposed over the years (e.g., whole suite [20], MIO [5], MOSA [38], or DynaMOSA [39]). Recent studies have shown that DYNAMOSA is more effective and efficient than other genetic algorithms for unit test generation of Java [12] and Python [28] programs.

Type Inference. A recent study by Gao et al. [22] showed that the lack of static types within JavaScript leads to bugs that could have been easily identified with a static type system. To combat this problem, various approaches have been proposed to infer/predict types for generating type annotations or assertions. Anderson et al. [4] proposed a formal approach for inferring types using constraint solvers based on a custom JavaScript-like language. Chandra et al. [13] proposed a formal type inference approach for static compilation of JavaScript programs. These approaches, however, only support a subset of the JavaScript syntax and, therefore, will not work on all programs. JSNice [41] and Deep-Typer [24] are two other approaches that train a model based on training data and use it to predict future type information. These approaches have the shortcoming that they can only predict basic JavaScript types. Meaning that they are unable to predict/assert user-defined types. Additionally, these approaches cannot consider the context of the literals and objects within a program or function. Type4Py [32] is a similar approach that uses a Deep Neural Network (DNN) to infer types for Python projects and suffers from similar limitations.

Testing for JavaScript. JavaScript started out as a client-side programming language for the browser. Most work related to testing for JavaScript is, therefore, also focused on web applications within the browser (e.g., [9,27,34,44]). Existing client-side testing approaches either focus on specific subsystems such as the browser's event handling system [9,27] or the interaction of JavaScript with the *Document Object Model* of the browser [34]. Nowadays, JavaScript is also a very commonly-used language for back-end development on *Node.js*. Tanida et al. [44] proposed a symbolic execution approach that uses a constraint solver for input data generation. Other approaches focused on mutation testing [33] or contract-based testing [23]. However, to the best of our knowledge, there exists no approach for automatic unit-level test case generation for JavaScript.

```
1   function example (a) {
2     if (a < 6) {
3       return 0
4     }
5     return a
6   }
```

(a) Example Code

1. $[L_R, example, a]$
2. $[L < R, a, 6]$
3. $[L \rightarrow R, example, 0]$
4. $[L \rightarrow R, example, a]$
5. $[L(R), example, 5]$

(b) Extracted Relations

Fig. 1. Extracting relations from code

3   Approach

This section details our test case generation approach for JavaScript programs that relies on Unsupervised Type Inference. Our approach consists of three phases, which are detailed in the next subsections.

3.1   Phase 1: Static Analysis

The first phase inspects the Subject Under Test (SUT) and its dependencies. First, this phase builds the Abstract Syntax Trees (ASTs) and extracts all identifiers and literals from the code; these will be referred to as *elements*. Afterward, the static analyzer extracts the relations between those elements and all user-defined objects, i.e., classes, interfaces, or prototyped objects.

Elements. As mentioned before, the elements consist of *identifiers* and *literals*. The former are the named references to variables, functions, and properties. The latter are constant values assigned to variables; examples are strings, numbers, and booleans. The types of the literal are straightforward and do not require inference. However, the identifiers do not have explicit types in dynamically typed languages like JavaScript. Hence, their types need to be inferred based on the *contextual* information (or *relations*) of the extracted elements.

Relations. Relations correspond to operations performed on code elements and describe how these elements are used and relate to other elements, providing hints on their types. For example, let us consider the *assignment* relation $L = R$, where R (right-hand element) is a boolean literal; we can logically derive (or infer) that L (left-hand element) must also be a boolean variable.

These relations are extracted from the AST and are converted to a consistent format that allows for easy identification of the relation type. Let us assume that there is a *lower than* relation between variable a and literal 6, as shown in Fig. 1a on line 2. This relation is converted and recorded as $[L < R, a, 6]$, as shown in Fig. 1b. In general, a relation is stored as a tuple containing (1) the type of operation ($L < R$ in our example) and (2) the list of operands (i.e., a and 6 in our example). The full list of extracted relations for the code snippet in Fig. 1a is reported in Fig. 1b.

```
const x = (a == b ? 6 : 10)
```

(a) Nested Relation

1. $[L = R, x, y*]$
2. $y* = [C?L : R, z*, 6, 10]$
3. $z* = [L == R, a, b]$

(b) Extracted Relations

Fig. 2. Extracting relations from nested code

In total, we designed 75 possible relations based on the MDN web documentation by Mozilla[3]. These operations/relations are classified into 15 categories, namely (1) *primary*, (2) *left-hand side*, (3) *increment/decrement*, (4) *unary*, (5) *arithmetic*, (6) *relational*, (7) *equality*, (8) *bitwise shift*, (9) *binary bitwise*, (10) *binary logical*, (11) *ternary*, (12) *optional chaining*, (13) *assignment*, (14) *comma*, and (15) *function* expressions. The complete list of relations is available in our replication package.

Nested relations are special types of relations whose composing elements are relations themselves. As an example, let us consider the code snippet in Fig. 2a. The corresponding relation for the assignment is $[L = R, x, y*]$, where y^* is an *artificial* element that points to the whole right-hand side of the assignment. This element corresponds to a ternary relation $[C?L : R, z*, 6, 10]$, which also includes an artificial element, called z^*, that points to the equality relation in the conditional part of the ternary statement. So z^* points to the final relation $[L == R, a, b]$. Although the code in Fig. 2a seems rather simple, it corresponds to three relations, two of which are nested, as shown in Fig. 2b.

Scopes. A critical aspect of the elements we have not yet discussed is scoping. The scope of an identifier determines its accessibility. To better understand the importance of the scope, let us consider the example in Fig. 3. First, the constant x is assigned the value 5. The constant x is defined in the so-called *global scope*. Next, a function is defined, creating a new scope. This scope has access to references of the global scope. Still, it can also have its own references, which are only available within its sub-scopes. In our example, another constant x is defined within the function scope. Note that from line 4, every reference to x in the scope of the function refers to the newly defined constant, not the x constant of the global scope. This type of operation is called *variable shadowing*. In a nutshell, variable shadowing is when the code contains an identifier for which there are multiple declarations in separate scopes. In these situations, the narrower scope *shadows* the other identifier declarations.

This shadowing principle is fundamental during the first phase of our approach because variables in the global scope are not the same variables as those in the function scope (e.g., x in Fig. 3). In fact, variables with the same identifier names but within different scopes can also have different types. In the example of Fig. 3, x from the global scope is numerical, while the x from the function scope is a string. In conclusion, the relations include the involved elements together with their scope.

---

[3] https://developer.mozilla.org/en-US/docs/Web/JavaScript/Reference/Operators.

```
1    const x = 5
2
3    function example(a) {
4        const x = "Hello "
5        return x + a
6    }
```

Fig. 3. Scopes

Complex Objects. In JavaScript, objects are the building blocks of the language and are stored as key-value pairs. Apart from primitive types like booleans and numbers, almost everything is represented as an object. An array, for example, is a special object where the keys are numbers. In recent JavaScript versions, developers can define classes and interfaces through a prototype-based object model, inducing a more object-oriented approach to JavaScript. Since these objects play such a prominent role in JavaScript, it is important that object types can be inferred as well. Hence, our approach extracts all object descriptions available in the program under test, including class, interface definitions, and standard objects (e.g., functions).

3.2 Phase 2: Unsupervised Static Type Inference

The second phase builds a probabilistic type model for the elements extracted from the first phase. For literal elements, the type inference is straightforward as the type can be directly inferred from the literal type. However, for non-literal elements, our probabilistic model considers all *type hints* that can be inferred from the relations extracted in the previous phase.

For example, the assignment x = 5 corresponds to the relation $[L = R, x, 5]$. From such a relation, we can derive that, at this particular point in the code, x must be numerical since it is assigned the literal value 5. However, for statements like x = y + z, there are various possibilities for the type of x depending the on types of y and z. To illustrate, the + operator can be applied to both numbers (arithmetic sum) and strings (string concatenation). Besides, in JavaScript, it is also possible to concatenate numbers with strings. For example, 1 + "1" returns the number 11. Therefore, multiple types can be assigned to elements that have relations/operations compatible with multiple data types.

To account for this, our model assigns scores to each type depending on the number of hints that can be derived for that type by its relations in the code. In general, given the element e and the set of relations $R = \{r_1, \ldots r_n\}$ associated to e as extracted from a program P, our model assigns each type t a score equal to the number of relations that can be applied to t (i.e., the number of hints):

$$score(e, t) = |hints(e, t)| \quad \text{where} \quad hints(e, t) = \{r_i \in R : r_i \text{ applies to } t\} \quad (1)$$

Finally, the element e has a probability of being assigned the type t proportional to the number of hints received for t:

$$p(e, t) = \frac{score(e, t)}{\sum_{t_i} score(e, t_i)} \tag{2}$$

The higher the score of a particular type, the larger the probability that the element is of that type. The probabilities are later used to sample argument types in the search phase.

For example, let us consider the statement x = y + z, which can be applied to both strings and numbers. In this case, our probabilistic model would assign +1 hint for numbers and +1 hint for strings. Hence, both types will have an equal probability of 50%.

Nested Types. The probability model takes into account both simple and nested relations. For example, let us consider the JavaScript statement: c = a > b. Such a statement corresponds to two relations (one of which is nested): $[l_i = R, o, d_*]$ and $d* = [L > R, a, b]$. The outcome for $d* = [L > R, a, b]$ is boolean no matter the types of a and b. Therefore, we can infer the variable (or element) c should be as well. Hence, the hints and scores are obtained by considering all relations, including the nested ones.

Resolving Complex Objects. Complex objects are characterized by *property accessor* relations, i.e., operations that aim to access properties of certain objects (e.g., using the dot notation object.property). If an element is involved in one or more *property accessor* relations, the accessed properties are compared to the available object descriptions. If there is an overlap between the element's properties and the properties of an object description, the object description receives +1 hint. In addition to matching object descriptions, an anonymous object type is created and assigned as a possible type. This anonymous object type exactly matches the properties of the element. This object is used when no other object matches are found.

3.3   Phase 3: Test Case Generation

The third phase generates test cases using meta-heuristics with the goal of maximizing branch coverage. As explained in Sect. 2, we use the Dynamic Many-Objective Sorting Algorithm (DynaMOSA) [39] as suggested in the literature [12,29,40]. Previous studies have shown that DYNAMOSA outperforms other meta-heuristics in unit test case generation for Java [12,40], python [29], and solidity [36] programs. Assessing other meta-heuristics in the context of unit test generations for JavaScript programs is part of our future agenda.

Our implementation applies the probabilistic model described in Sect. 3.2 to determine what is the potential type of each input parameter. We have implemented two different strategies to incorporate the type inference model into the main DYNAMOSA loop, namely *proportional type sampling* and *ranking*.

Table 1. Benchmark statistics

Benchmark	#Units	CC	SLOC	Avg. n. branches
Commander.js	4	23	208	29
Express	15	20	222	25
Moment.js	54	7	33	8
Javascript Algorithms	30	5	68	8
Lodash	10	11	63	16

Proportional Sampling. This strategy can assign various types to each input parameter. As explained in Sect. 3.2, our model assigns scores to multiple types (see Eq. (1)) based on the number of positive hints received by analyzing the associated relations. When creating a new test case (either in the initial population or during mutation), each input parameter is assigned one of the types. Each candidate type has a probability of being selected equal to the value obtained by applying Eq. (2). Notice that each data type is sampled for each newly generated test case. Therefore, the same input parameter (for the same function) may be assigned different types every time a new test case is created.

Ranking. This strategy assigns only one type to the input parameter. In particular, this strategy sorts all types with positive hints in descending order of their score values. Then, this method selects the type with the largest probability (or the largest number of hints).

Test Execution. Once generated, each generated test case will contain a sequence of function calls with their input data. These tests are then executed against the program under test, and the coverage information is stored. The "fitness" of a test is measured according to its distance to cover all unreached branches in the code, as typically done in DYNAMOSA. The distance to each uncovered branch is computed using two well-known coverage heuristics [31]: (1) the *approach level* and (2) the normalized *branch distance*.

4   Empirical Study

To assess the impact of the unsupervised probabilistic type inference on the performance of search-based unit test generation for JavaScript, we perform an empirical evaluation to answer the following research questions:

RQ1 *How does unsupervised static type inference impact structural coverage of* DYNAMOSA *for JavaScript?*
RQ2 *What is the best strategy to incorporate type inference in* DYNAMOSA*?*

Benchmark. To the best of our knowledge, there is no existing JavaScript benchmark for unit-level test case generation. Hence, for our empirical study, we build a benchmark comprising of five JavaScript projects: *Express*[4], *Commander.js*[5], *Moment.js*[6], *JavaScript Algorithms*[7], *Lodash*[8]. These projects were selected based on their popularity in the JavaScript community (measured through the number of stars on GitHub) and represent a diverse collection of JavaScript syntax and code styles. From these projects, we selected a subset of units (*i.e.*, classes or functions) based on two criteria: (1) the unit has to be testable (*i.e.*, the unit has to be exported), and (2) the unit needs to be non-trivial (*i.e.*, have a Cyclomatic Complexity of $CC \geq 2$ as calculated by *Plato*[9]). The latter criterion is in line with existing guidelines for assessing test case generation tools [40]. Table 1 provides the main characteristics of our benchmark at the project-level, including the average Cyclomatic Complexity per project (**CC** column), the average Source Lines Of Code (**SLOC** column), and the average number of branches. It is worth noting that some of the files in the selected projects had to be excluded or modified. For example, in the `Commander.js` project there are two files that contain statements that terminate the running process. This has the effect of also terminating the test case generation process. Therefore, we have excluded this file from the benchmark and modified it, so that any other files depending on it will not be affected.

Prototype. To evaluate the proposed approach, we have developed a prototype for unit-level test case generation that implements our unsupervised dynamic type inference, written in `Typescript`. The prototype also implements the state-of-the-art search algorithm for test case generation, namely DYNAMOSA [39], as well as the guiding heuristics [31], i.e., the approach level and branch distance.

Parameter Settings. For this study, we have chosen to mainly adopt the default search algorithm parameter values as described in literature [39]. Previous studies have shown that although parameter tuning impacts the search algorithm's performance, the default parameter values provide reasonable and acceptable results [8]. Hence, the search algorithm uses a single point crossover with a crossover probability of 0.75, mutation with a probability of $1/n$ ($n =$ number of statements in the test case), and tournament selection. For the population size, however, we decided to deviate from the default (50). We went for a size of 30 as our preliminary experiment showed this worked best for a benchmark this size. The search budget per unit under test is 60 s. This is a common value used in related work [35].

Experimental Protocol. To answer RQ1, we compare the two variants of our approach with DYNAMOSA without type inference. In particular, for this baseline, the type for the input data is randomly sampled among all types that can be extracted using the relations described in Sect. 3.1. To answer RQ2, we

---

[4] https://expressjs.com/.
[5] https://tj.github.io/commander.js/.
[6] https://momentjs.com/.
[7] https://github.com/trekhleb/javascript-algorithms.
[8] https://lodash.com/.
[9] https://github.com/es-analysis/plato.

compare the two variants of our approach: (1) proportional type sampling, and (2) ranking.

To account for the stochastic nature of the approach, each unit under test was run 20 times. We performed 20 repetitions of 3 configurations (*i.e.,* random type sampling, ranking, and proportional sampling) on 98 units under test, for a total of 5880 runs. This required $(5880 \text{ runs} \times 60\,\text{s})/(60\,\text{s} \times 60\,\text{min} \times 24\,\text{h}) \approx 4.1\,\text{d}$ computation time. At the end of each run, we stored the maximum branch coverage achieved by the approach for the active configuration (**RQ1** and **RQ2**). The experiment was performed on a system with an AMD Ryzen 9 3900X (12 cores 3.8 GHz) with 32 GB of RAM. Each experiment was given a maximum of 8 GB of RAM. To determine if one approach performs better than the others, we applied the unpaired Wilcoxon signed-rank test [16] with a threshold of 0.05. This non-parametric statistical test determines if two data distributions are significantly different. In addition, we apply the Vargha-Delaney $\hat{A}_{12}$ statistic [45] to determine the effect size of the result, which determines the magnitude of the difference between the two data distributions.

5   Results

This section discusses the results of our empirical study with the aim of answering the research questions formulated in Sect. 4. All differences in results are presented in absolute differences (percentage points).

Result for RQ1: Structural Coverage. Table 2 summarizes the results achieved by our approach on the benchmark with the winning configuration highlighted in gray color. It shows the median branch coverage and the Inter-Quartile-Range (IQR) for the two possible strategies to incorporate the type inference model (Ranking, Proportional) and a baseline that uses random type sampling (Random). The *Units* column indicates the number of units (*i.e.,* exported classes and functions) that are tested in the file of the benchmark project.

On average for all 57 files in the benchmark, *random* achieves 33.4% branch coverage, *ranking* 42.7%, and *proportional type sampling* 46.0%. The baseline still performs quite well, as *random type sampling* can be effective in triggering assertion branches and can over time guess the correct types for primitives. For the *ranking* strategy, the average improvement in branch coverage is 9.3%. The file with the least improvement is `suggestSimilar.js` from the `Commander.js` project with an average decrease of 13%. The file with the most improvement is `add-subtract.js` from the `Moment.js` project with an average increase of 71%, which corresponds to 10 additionally covered branches. For the *proportional* strategy, the average improvement in branch coverage is 12.6%. There are 24 files for which the *proportional* strategy performs equally to the baseline. The file with the most improvement is again `add-subtract.js` from the `Moment.js` project with an average increase of 71%.

Table 3 shows the results of the statistical comparison between the two strategies and the baseline, based on a *p*-value ≤ 0.05. *#Win* indicates the number of

Table 2. Median branch coverage and the inter-quartile-range. The largest values are highlighted in gray color.

Benchmark	File Name	#Units	Random		Ranking		Proportional	
			Median	IQR	Median	IQR	Median	IQR
Commander.js	help.js	1	0.20	0.019	0.41	0.076	0.53	0.023
	option.js	2	0.33	0.056	0.33	0.056	0.39	0.000
	suggestSimilar.js	1	0.69	0.062	0.56	0.156	0.75	0.062
Express	application.js	1	0.63	0.019	0.63	0.019	0.65	0.019
	query.js	1	0.67	0.000	0.67	0.000	0.67	0.000
	request.js	1	0.25	0.000	0.27	0.023	0.25	0.023
	response.js	1	0.14	0.007	0.13	0.013	0.14	0.013
	utils.js	7	0.56	0.007	0.62	0.000	0.59	0.029
	view.js	1	0.06	0.000	0.06	0.000	0.06	0.000
JS Algorithms Graph	articulationPoints.js	1	0.00	0.000	0.00	0.000	0.08	0.000
	bellmanFord.js	1	0.00	0.000	0.17	0.000	0.33	0.000
	bfTravellingSalesman.js	1	0.00	0.000	0.08	0.000	0.08	0.000
	breadthFirstSearch.js	1	0.12	0.125	0.38	0.031	0.31	0.125
	depthFirstSearch.js	1	0.00	0.167	0.00	0.167	0.00	0.167
	detectDirectedCycle.js	1	0.00	0.000	0.12	0.000	0.38	0.000
	dijkstra.js	1	0.00	0.000	0.10	0.000	0.20	0.100
	eulerianPath.js	1	0.00	0.000	0.00	0.000	0.21	0.000
	floydWarshall.js	1	0.00	0.000	0.67	0.000	0.67	0.000
	hamiltonianCycle.js	1	0.00	0.000	0.00	0.000	0.00	0.050
	kruskal.js	1	0.10	0.100	0.30	0.000	0.30	0.000
	prim.js	1	0.08	0.000	0.08	0.083	0.17	0.000
	stronglyConnectedComponents.js	1	0.00	0.000	0.00	0.000	0.25	0.000
JS Algorithms Knapsack	Knapsack.js	1	0.57	0.000	0.50	0.000	0.57	0.000
	KnapsackItem.js	1	0.50	0.000	0.50	0.000	0.50	0.000
JS Algorithms Matrix	Matrix.js	12	0.79	0.053	0.74	0.026	0.80	0.158
JS Algorithms Sort	CountingSort.js	1	0.92	0.083	0.92	0.021	0.92	0.000
JS Algorithms Tree	RedBlackTree.js	1	0.21	0.000	0.26	0.000	0.29	0.037
Lodash	equalArrays.js	1	0.08	0.000	0.67	0.042	0.75	0.052
	hasPath.js	1	0.75	0.156	0.75	0.000	0.88	0.250
	random.js	1	1.00	0.000	1.00	0.000	1.00	0.000
	result.js	1	0.90	0.100	0.80	0.000	0.90	0.100
	slice.js	1	1.00	0.000	1.00	0.000	1.00	0.000
	split.js	1	0.88	0.000	0.88	0.000	0.88	0.000
	toNumber.js	1	0.60	0.000	0.65	0.000	0.65	0.050
	transform.js	1	0.83	0.000	0.83	0.000	0.83	0.083
	truncate.js	1	0.38	0.000	0.59	0.029	0.59	0.000
	unzip.js	1	1.00	0.000	1.00	0.000	1.00	0.000
Moment.js	add-subtract.js	1	0.00	0.000	0.71	0.018	0.71	0.000
	calendar.js	2	0.05	0.000	0.45	0.091	0.43	0.091
	check-overflow.js	1	0.05	0.000	0.60	0.000	0.60	0.000
	compare.js	6	0.14	0.000	0.14	0.000	0.14	0.000
	constructor.js	3	0.38	0.000	0.53	0.008	0.41	0.156
	date-from-array.js	2	0.88	0.000	0.88	0.000	0.88	0.000
	format.js	4	0.08	0.000	0.08	0.000	0.08	0.000
	from-anything.js	2	0.68	0.059	0.71	0.000	0.69	0.037
	from-array.js	1	0.02	0.000	0.04	0.000	0.04	0.000
	from-object.js	1	0.50	0.000	0.50	0.000	0.50	0.000
	from-string-and-array.js	1	0.00	0.000	0.31	0.000	0.31	0.000
	from-string-and-format.js	1	0.06	0.000	0.56	0.039	0.55	0.133
	from-string.js	3	0.06	0.000	0.16	0.000	0.16	0.000
	get-set.js	5	0.14	0.000	0.23	0.045	0.36	0.068
	locale.js	2	0.17	0.167	0.17	0.000	0.17	0.000
	min-max.js	2	0.12	0.000	0.12	0.000	0.12	0.000
	now.js	1	0.50	0.000	0.50	0.000	0.50	0.000
	parsing-flags.js	1	0.50	0.000	0.50	0.125	0.50	0.000
	start-end-of.js	2	0.10	0.000	0.10	0.000	0.10	0.000
	valid.js	2	0.38	0.000	0.38	0.000	0.38	0.000

Table 3. Statistical results w.r.t. branch coverage

Comparison	#Win				#No diff.	#Lose			
	Negl.	Small	Medium	Large	Negl.	Negl.	Small	Medium	Large
Ranking vs. Random	-	3	1	23	26	-	1	-	3
Prop. sampling vs. Random	-	1	4	27	25	-	-	-	-
Prop. sampling vs. Ranking	-	4	-	16	33	-	3	1	-

times that the left configuration has a statistically significant improvement over the right one. *#No diff.* indicates the number of times that there is no evidence that the two competing configurations are different; *#Lose* indicates the number of times that the left configuration has statistically worse results than the right one. The *#Win* and *#Lose* columns also include the $\hat{A}_{12}$ effect size, classified into *Small, Medium, Large,* and *Negligible*.

We can see that the *ranking* and the *proportional* strategy have a statistically significant non-negligible improvement over the baseline in 27 and 32 files for branch coverage, respectively. *Ranking* improves with a large magnitude for 23 classes, medium for 1 class, and small for 3 classes and *proportional* with 27 (large), 4 (medium), and 1 (small). The *Ranking* strategy loses in four cases when compared to the baseline: `response.js`, `response.js`, `Knapsack.js`, `Matrix.js`, and `results.js`.

Result for RQ2: Strategy. When we compare the two different strategies with each other, we can observe that the *proportional type inference* on average improves by 3.3% over the *ranked* strategy based on branch coverage. The file with the least improvement is `constructor.js` from the `Moment.js` project with an average decrease of 12%. While the file with the most improvement is `detectDirectedCycle.js` from the `JS Algorithms` project with an average increase of 36%. From Table 3, we can see that the *proportional* strategy has a statistically significant non-negligible improvement over *ranking* in 20 cases (16 large and 4 small). While *ranking* improves over *proportional* in only 4 cases (1 medium and 3 small): `slice.js`, `constructor.js`, `from-string-and-format.js`, and `parsing-flags.js`.

6   Threats to Validity

This section discusses the potential threats to the validity of our study.

External Validity: An important threat regards the generalizability of our study. We selected five open-source projects based on their popularity in the JavaScript community. The projects are diverse in terms of size, application domain, purpose, syntax, and code style. Further experiments on a larger set of projects would increase the confidence in the generalizability of our study and, therefore, is part of our future work.

Conclusion Validity: Threats to *conclusion validity* are related to the randomized nature of DynaMOSA. To minimize this risk, we have executed each configuration 20 times with different random seeds. We have followed the best practices for running experiments with randomized algorithms as laid out in well-established guidelines [7]. Additionally, we used the unpaired Wilcoxon signed-rank test and the Vargha-Delaney $\hat{A}_{12}$ effect size to assess the significance and magnitude of our results. To ensure a controlled environment that provides a fair evaluation, all experiments have been conducted on the same system and interfering processes were kept to a minimum.

7 Conclusion and Future Work

In this paper, we presented an automated unit test generation approach for JavaScript, the most popular dynamically-typed language. It generates unit-level test cases by using the state-of-the-art meta-heuristic search algorithm DYNAMOSA and a novel unsupervised probabilistic type inference model. Our results show that (1) the proposed approach can successfully generate test cases for well-established libraries in JavaScript, and (2) the type inference model plays a significant role in achieving larger code coverage (through *proportional sampling*). As part of our future work, we plan (1) to extend our benchmark, (2) to investigate more meta-heuristics, (3) assess different strategies to incorporate the type inference model within the search process, and (4) compare our type inference model to state-of-the-art deep learning approaches.

References

1. Abdessalem, R.B., Panichella, A., Nejati, S., Briand, L.C., Stifter, T.: Testing autonomous cars for feature interaction failures using many-objective search. In: 2018 33rd IEEE/ACM International Conference on Automated Software Engineering (ASE), pp. 143–154 (2018)
2. Almasi, M.M., Hemmati, H., Fraser, G., Arcuri, A., Benefelds, J.: An industrial evaluation of unit test generation: finding real faults in a financial application. In: 2017 IEEE/ACM 39th International Conference on Software Engineering: Software Engineering in Practice Track (ICSE-SEIP), pp. 263–272 (2017)
3. Alshahwan, N., et al.: Deploying search based software engineering with Sapienz at Facebook. In: Colanzi, T.E., McMinn, P. (eds.) SSBSE 2018. LNCS, vol. 11036, pp. 3–45. Springer, Cham (2018). https://doi.org/10.1007/978-3-319-99241-9_1
4. Anderson, C., Giannini, P., Drossopoulou, S.: Towards type inference for JavaScript. In: Black, A.P. (ed.) ECOOP 2005. LNCS, vol. 3586, pp. 428–452. Springer, Heidelberg (2005). https://doi.org/10.1007/11531142_19
5. Arcuri, A.: Test suite generation with the many independent objective (MIO) algorithm. Inf. Softw. Technol. **104**, 195–206 (2018)
6. Arcuri, A.: RESTful API automated test case generation with EvoMaster. ACM Trans. Softw. Eng. Methodol. (TOSEM) **28**(1), 1–37 (2019)
7. Arcuri, A., Briand, L.: A hitchhiker's guide to statistical tests for assessing randomized algorithms in software engineering. Softw. Test. Verif. Reliab. **24**(3), 219–250 (2014)

8. Arcuri, A., Fraser, G.: Parameter tuning or default values? An empirical investigation in search-based software engineering. Empir. Softw. Eng. **18**(3), 594–623 (2013)

9. Artzi, S., Dolby, J., Jensen, S.H., Møller, A., Tip, F.: A framework for automated testing of JavaScript web applications. In: Proceedings of the 33rd International Conference on Software Engineering, pp. 571–580 (2011)

10. Baldoni, R., Coppa, E., D'elia, D.C., Demetrescu, C., Finocchi, I.: A survey of symbolic execution techniques. ACM Comput. Surv. (CSUR) **51**(3), 1–39 (2018)

11. Ben Abdessalem, R., Nejati, S., Briand, L.C., Stifter, T.: Testing advanced driver assistance systems using multi-objective search and neural networks. In: Proceedings of the 31st IEEE/ACM International Conference on Automated Software Engineering, pp. 63–74 (2016)

12. Campos, J., Ge, Y., Albunian, N., Fraser, G., Eler, M., Arcuri, A.: An empirical evaluation of evolutionary algorithms for unit test suite generation. Inf. Softw. Technol. **104**, 207–235 (2018)

13. Chandra, S., et al.: Type inference for static compilation of JavaScript. ACM SIGPLAN Not. **51**(10), 410–429 (2016)

14. Chen, T.Y., Leung, H., Mak, I.K.: Adaptive random testing. In: Maher, M.J. (ed.) ASIAN 2004. LNCS, vol. 3321, pp. 320–329. Springer, Heidelberg (2004). https://doi.org/10.1007/978-3-540-30502-6_23

15. Clarke, L.A.: A system to generate test data and symbolically execute programs. IEEE Trans. Software Eng. **3**, 215–222 (1976)

16. Conover, W.J.: Practical Nonparametric Statistics, vol. 350. Wiley, Hoboken (1998)

17. Derakhshanfar, P., Devroey, X., Panichella, A., Zaidman, A., van Deursen, A.: Towards integration-level test case generation using call site information. arXiv preprint arXiv:2001.04221 (2020)

18. Fraser, G., Arcuri, A.: EvoSuite: automatic test suite generation for object-oriented software. In: Proceedings of the 19th ACM SIGSOFT Symposium and the 13th European Conference on Foundations of Software Engineering, pp. 416–419 (2011)

19. Fraser, G., Arcuri, A.: EvoSuite: automatic test suite generation for object-oriented software. In: Proceedings of the 19th ACM SIGSOFT Symposium and the 13th European Conference on Foundations of Software Engineering, ESEC/FSE 2011, pp. 416–419. ACM, New York (2011). https://doi.org/10.1145/2025113.2025179

20. Fraser, G., Arcuri, A.: Whole test suite generation. IEEE Trans. Softw. Eng. **39**(2), 276–291 (2012)

21. Fraser, G., Arcuri, A.: 1600 faults in 100 projects: automatically finding faults while achieving high coverage with EvoSuite. Empir. Softw. Eng. **20**(3), 611–639 (2015)

22. Gao, Z., Bird, C., Barr, E.T.: To type or not to type: quantifying detectable bugs in JavaScript. In: 2017 IEEE/ACM 39th International Conference on Software Engineering (ICSE), pp. 758–769 (2017)

23. Heidegger, P., Thiemann, P.: Contract-driven testing of JavaScript code. In: Vitek, J. (ed.) TOOLS 2010. LNCS, vol. 6141, pp. 154–172. Springer, Heidelberg (2010). https://doi.org/10.1007/978-3-642-13953-6_9

24. Hellendoorn, V.J., Bird, C., Barr, E.T., Allamanis, M.: Deep learning type inference. In: Proceedings of the 2018 26th ACM Joint Meeting on European Software Engineering Conference and Symposium on the Foundations of Software Engineering, pp. 152–162 (2018)

25. Kifetew, F., Devroey, X., Rueda, U.: Java unit testing tool competition-seventh round. In: 2019 IEEE/ACM 12th International Workshop on Search-Based Software Testing (SBST), pp. 15–20 (2019)

26. Lakhotia, K., Harman, M., Gross, H.: AUSTIN: an open source tool for search based software testing of c programs. Inf. Softw. Technol. **55**(1), 112–125 (2013)
27. Li, G., Andreasen, E., Ghosh, I.: SymJS: automatic symbolic testing of JavaScript web applications. In: Proceedings of the 22nd ACM SIGSOFT International Symposium on Foundations of Software Engineering, pp. 449–459 (2014)
28. Lukasczyk, S., Kroiß, F., Fraser, G.: Automated unit test generation for Python. In: Aleti, A., Panichella, A. (eds.) SSBSE 2020. LNCS, vol. 12420, pp. 9–24. Springer, Cham (2020). https://doi.org/10.1007/978-3-030-59762-7_2
29. Lukasczyk, S., Kroiß, F., Fraser, G.: An empirical study of automated unit test generation for python. arXiv preprint arXiv:2111.05003 (2021)
30. Matinnejad, R., Nejati, S., Briand, L.C., Bruckmann, T.: Automated test suite generation for time-continuous simulink models. In: proceedings of the 38th International Conference on Software Engineering, pp. 595–606 (2016)
31. McMinn, P.: Search-based software test data generation: a survey. Softw. Test. Verif. Reliab. **14**(2), 105–156 (2004)
32. Mir, A.M., Latoškinas, E., Proksch, S., Gousios, G.: Type4Py: practical deep similarity learning-based type inference for Python. In: 2022 IEEE/ACM 44th International Conference on Software Engineering (ICSE), pp. 2241–2252 (2022)
33. Mirshokraie, S., Mesbah, A., Pattabiraman, K.: Efficient JavaScript mutation testing. In: 2013 IEEE Sixth International Conference on Software Testing, Verification and Validation, pp. 74–83 (2013)
34. Mirshokraie, S., Mesbah, A., Pattabiraman, K.: JSeft: automated JavaScript unit test generation. In: 2015 IEEE 8th International Conference on Software Testing, Verification and Validation (ICST), pp. 1–10 (2015)
35. Olsthoorn, M., van Deursen, A., Panichella, A.: Generating highly-structured input data by combining search-based testing and grammar-based fuzzing. In: 2020 35th IEEE/ACM International Conference on Automated Software Engineering (ASE), pp. 1224–1228 (2020)
36. Olsthoorn, M., Stallenberg, D., van Deursen, A., Panichella, A.: SynTest-solidity: automated test case generation and fuzzing for smart contracts. In: The 44th International Conference on Software Engineering-Demonstration Track (2022)
37. Panichella, A., Panichella, S., Fraser, G., Sawant, A.A., Hellendoorn, V.: Test smells 20 years later: detectability, validity, and reliability. Empir. Softw. Eng. **27**(7) (2022). https://doi.org/10.1007/s10664-022-10207-5
38. Panichella, A., Kifetew, F.M., Tonella, P.: Reformulating branch coverage as a many-objective optimization problem. In: 2015 IEEE 8th International Conference on Software Testing, Verification and Validation (ICST), pp. 1–10 (2015)
39. Panichella, A., Kifetew, F.M., Tonella, P.: Automated test case generation as a many-objective optimisation problem with dynamic selection of the targets. IEEE Trans. Softw. Eng. **44**(2), 122–158 (2017)
40. Panichella, A., Kifetew, F.M., Tonella, P.: A large scale empirical comparison of state-of-the-art search-based test case generators. Inf. Softw. Technol. **104**, 236–256 (2018)
41. Raychev, V., Vechev, M., Krause, A.: Predicting program properties from "big code". ACM SIGPLAN Not. **50**(1), 111–124 (2015)
42. Soltani, M., Panichella, A., Van Deursen, A.: Search-based crash reproduction and its impact on debugging. IEEE Trans. Softw. Eng. **46**(12), 1294–1317 (2018)
43. Stallenberg, D., Olsthoorn, M., Panichella, A.: Replication package of "guess what: test case generation for Javascript with unsupervised probabilistic type inference" (2022). https://doi.org/10.5281/zenodo.7088684

44. Tanida, H., Uehara, T., Li, G., Ghosh, I.: Automated unit testing of JavaScript code through symbolic executor SymJS. Int. J. Adv. Softw. **8**(1), 146–155 (2015)
45. Vargha, A., Delaney, H.D.: A critique and improvement of the CL common language effect size statistics of McGraw and Wong. J. Educ. Behav. Stati. **25**(2), 101–132 (2000)

EvoAttack: An Evolutionary Search-Based Adversarial Attack for Object Detection Models

Kenneth Chan$^{(\boxtimes)}$ and Betty H. C. Cheng

Department of Computer Science and Engineering, Michigan State University,
428 S Shaw Ln, East Lansing, MI 48824, USA
{chanken1,chengb}@msu.edu

Abstract. State-of-the-art deep neural networks in image classification, recognition, and detection tasks are increasingly being used in a range of real-world applications. Applications include those that are safety critical, where the failure of the system may cause serious harm, injuries, or even deaths. Adversarial examples are expected inputs that are maliciously modified such that the machine learning models fail to classify them correctly. While a number of evolutionary search-based approaches have been developed to generate adversarial examples against image classification problems, evolutionary search-based attacks against object detection algorithms remain unexplored. This paper explores how evolutionary search-based techniques can be used as a black-box, model- and data- agnostic approach to attack state-of-the-art object detection algorithms (e.g., RetinaNet and Faster R-CNN). A proof-of-concept implementation is provided to demonstrate how evolutionary search can generate adversarial examples that existing models fail to correctly process. We applied our approach to benchmark datasets, Microsoft COCO and Waymo Open Dataset, applying minor perturbations to generate adversarial examples that prevented correct model detections and classifications on areas of interest.

Keywords: Evolutionary search · Adversarial examples · Machine learning

1 Introduction

Many popular machine learning techniques, such as Deep Neural Networks (DNNs), are susceptible to carefully crafted malicious inputs [3,17]. These malicious inputs are known as *adversarial examples* [17]. DNNs are artificial neural networks with multiple layers of activation neurons that can be used for feature learning. DNNs have numerous real-world applications, such as malicious file detection [19,21], fraud detection [11,24], and autonomous vehicles [6,26]. In safety-critical systems [5], commercially-deployed DNNs may have significant consequences should they fail, leading to potential injury, serious harm, death,

© The Author(s), under exclusive license to Springer Nature Switzerland AG 2022
M. Papadakis and S. R. Vergilio (Eds.): SSBSE 2022, LNCS 13711, pp. 83–97, 2022.
https://doi.org/10.1007/978-3-031-21251-2_6

and/or financial loss. To prevent serious harm or injuries, DNNs deployed in safety-critical systems must be robust against adversarial attacks. Therefore, a challenge is how machine learning model robustness can be assessed and improved to correctly process inputs in the face of adversarial attacks. This paper introduces EVOATTACK, a black-box evolutionary search-based technique, to assess the robustness of object detection algorithms against a diverse collection of adversarial examples.

Over the past decade, several research efforts have addressed adversarial examples for image classification techniques [3,13,17,18]. Adversarial examples are expected input data (often part of the original dataset) with a small amount of human-imperceptible perturbations introduced to cause model failure (e.g., misclassification of class labels) [3,17]. Adversarial example research has largely focused on techniques that challenge the robustness of image classification techniques (i.e., given an image of an object, correctly label the object). However, object detection techniques (i.e., given an image with up to n number of objects, correctly identify the object(s) by drawing a bounding box around them and label them accordingly) have had limited research [25,28,29]. Compared to image classification, attacking object detection techniques is significantly more difficult as the images are larger in size, contain more dimensions, and contain multiple numbers of potential objects. Existing techniques for generating adversarial examples against object detection algorithms [25,28] assume a white-box model, where sensitive or critical model parameters are known to the adversary. While existing approaches can be used as weak black-box attacks (i.e., transfer from a white-box attack to a black-box model with similar architectures), such approaches often involve additional training overhead to produce a surrogate model to attack. As such, a true black-box, model- and data- agnostic approach (i.e., does not depend on model or data specific information) for object detection algorithms is still needed. Furthermore, while black-box approaches have been applied to image classification [12,23], they typically introduce a large amount of visible perturbation when applied to images with large dimensions.

As a means to assess model robustness against adversarial attacks, this paper introduces a black-box evolutionary search-based testing technique, EVOATTACK, to generate adversarial examples to compromise object detection algorithms by adversely impacting the detection of objects. The evolutionary search-based adversarial attack used in this work does not require access or estimates of hidden model parameters or model architecture, does not require additional training of surrogate models, and is model and data agnostic. This work contributes two key insights. First, we leverage the output of the object detection model in the previous generation to guide the mutation process and the structure of the fitness function. Second, we propose an adaptive mutation scheme that dynamically scales the mutation rate to reduce perturbation while promoting convergence.

Two key strategies are used to enable our approach to generate adversarial examples while minimizing human-perceptible perturbations. To generate adversarial examples, we use a generational Genetic Algorithm (GA), where individuals in a population evolve towards a global optimum (i.e., a perturbed image that adversely impacts model detection). Compared to image classification problems, object detection images contain multiple classification sub-problems. As such, we developed a fitness function that simultaneously accounts for all objects detected by the model during the inference stage. Specifically, the output of the model in the previous generation enables our approach to localize the perturbation region by ignoring pixels that do not directly affect the output of the model. Additionally, our fitness function dynamically adapts based on the number of bounding boxes and confidence scores from the previous generation's detections. During mutation, we apply a fine-grained approach for generating perturbation by focusing on pixels in areas of interest. We introduce an adaptive mutation scheme, where we promote minor perturbations for each object in the image, while encouraging misdetection from the model. In the proposed adaptive mutation scheme, we mutate a small number of pixels when the generation count is low. In order to promote convergence, the number of modified pixels is dynamically scaled up as the number of generations increases.

In our experiments, we verify that EVOATTACK can produce adversarial examples that prevent object detection. We implemented the proposed approach and generated adversarial examples against existing object detection models, such as RetinaNet [10] and Faster R-CNN [20]. To illustrate the potential impact of adversarial examples against object detection models, we apply our technique to attack a set of images obtained from the Microsoft COCO dataset [14] and the Waymo Open Dataset [16] to show how adversarial examples can be generated against two different benchmark datasets. Preliminary results show that our algorithm can cause the model to deviate from the expected output, while maintaining a low degree of visible perturbations (i.e., L0 and L2 norms). This work shows that black-box evolutionary search-based adversarial examples can be generated against object detection tasks, a domain not yet explored to the best of our knowledge. The remainder of this paper is organized as follows. Section 2 overviews background material and reviews related work. Next, Sect. 3 describes the details of the proposed approach. Section 4 describes the validation work of our approach. Finally, Sect. 5 concludes the paper and discusses future directions.

2   Background

This section provides background information for the paper. First, we describe adversarial examples. Next, we compare the image classification problem with the object detection problem. Finally, we overview related work.

2.1   Adversarial Examples

Adversarial examples describe machine learning model inputs that are maliciously perturbed to cause a failure in the model. Figure 1 shows an example of an adversarial example. The original input image (i.e., an image with the corresponding identified objects) is shown on the left. When the malicious perturbation noise (scaled by a factor of 10 for readability purposes) is added to the input image, the resulting image prevents the detection of the objects. Adversarial examples closely resemble original images, and thus are not human distinguishable.

Different adversaries may have different types of access and understanding of the underlying model's architecture and parameters. *White-box* attacks assume that the adversary has access to sensitive information of the model [29]. For example, the adversary may have information about the type of model, weights, gradient information, and/or the architecture of the model. Traditional attack methods such as L-BFGS [17], Fast Gradient Sign Method (FGSM) [3], and Dense Adversary Generation (DAG) [28] exploit gradient information of the model to be attacked and modify the image by inducing noise based on the gradient information. In contrast, *black-box* attacks assume that the adversary has no prior knowledge of the model to be attacked [29]. The adversary has access to a compiled model and may query the model with any input to obtain the model's output, but does not have access to the underlying weights and architecture of the model. Thus, a black-box attack closely resembles a real-world attack scenario where the development of the DNN model may be proprietary, and only the compiled model is publicly available.

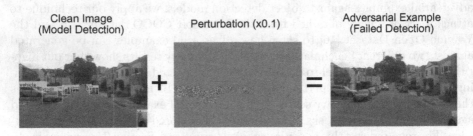

Clean Image
(Model Detection)

Perturbation (x0.1)

Adversarial Example
(Failed Detection)

Fig. 1. Example of an adversarial example, where the original clean input with malicious perturbations prevents model detection.

2.2   Adversarial Examples for Object Detection Algorithms

Compared to the image classification problem, object detection is an inherently more difficult problem for both model inference and attacks [28]. In image classification, an input image consists of exactly one object. The model returns a prediction label with a confidence score, denoting the probability that the object is of the corresponding label. Since the input consists of one object, every pixel in the image may contribute to the output of the model. In object detection algorithms, input images are often large in dimensions with multiple objects of interest. The objective of the model is to correctly identify objects in the image, draw bounding boxes, and provide the object types. Thus, most regions of the input image may not contribute to the output of the model. If we allow all pixels of the image to be mutated, then the objective of minimal perturbations of adversarial examples may not be satisfied. As such, alternative approaches for selecting the perturbation space must be developed for attacking object detection algorithms.

2.3 Related Work

This section overviews related work in the area of adversarial examples, black-box approaches, and current research for adversarial examples applied to object detection. While other works have explored evolutionary search-based adversarial examples for classification problems, this paper examines how evolutionary search-based approaches can be used to attack object detection algorithms.

Szegedy et al. [17] introduced the first adversarial examples, revealing the existence of malicious images that machine learning models fail to predict correctly. Carlini and Wagner [1] introduced the C&W attack similar to that of Szegedy et al.'s attack [17]. Goodfellow et al. [3] proposed the FGSM algorithm to perturb the image based on the signed gradient. However, most of the adversarial example generation techniques explore white-box attacks, where the gradient and other sensitive information of the underlying model are not hidden from the adversary. Our approach assumes a black-box model where the adversary does not have access to model weights and architecture.

Several researchers have explored the use of black-box evolutionary approaches to generate adversarial examples for image classification algorithms, but to the best of our knowledge, these techniques have not targeted object detection algorithms. Su et al. [22] proposed a one-pixel attack using Differential Evolution (DE). Alzantot et al. [12] proposed GenAttack, which applies a variation of GA to discover adversarial examples. Vidnerová et al. [23], Chen et al. [2], Wu et al. [27], and Han et al. [4] proposed similar GA approaches. These approaches use different evolutionary search techniques (e.g., evolutionary algorithms, GAs, multi-objective GAs, etc.) and target different applications and datasets.

Finally, a number of research efforts have explored generating adversarial examples against object detection models. Xie et al. [28] proposed the DAG algorithm that calculates the gradients with respect to all correctly-labeled objects and accumulates perturbations that reduce the model's output confidence. The authors applied their technique to previous state-of-the-art networks, such as the FCN framework and Faster R-CNN [20] on the PascalVOC dataset. In contrast, Wei et al. [25] proposed a transfer-based attack based on a Generative Adversarial Network (GAN). However, their approach requires the training of a surrogate model, thus resulting in additional training overhead. Furthermore, transferability attacks do not guarantee success. As such, current existing state-of-the-art techniques do not provide a true black-box, model- and data-agnostic approach for object detection algorithms.

3 Methodology

This section introduces our proposed evolutionary search-based approach to attack object detection algorithms. We first describe the image datasets used in our experiments. Next, we overview how we use evolutionary search to generate adversarial examples with the objective of minimizing perturbations. Finally, we introduce an adaptive mutation scheme that reduces the number of changed pixels and the degree of perturbations in adversarial examples.

3.1   Object Detection Benchmark Datasets

This work uses two benchmark datasets to validate the proposed technique to illustrate that evolutionary search-based attacks are not model or dataset-dependent. First, the Common Object in Context (COCO) [14] dataset is a large-scale dataset created by Microsoft to promote machine learning progress in object detection, segmentation, and captioning. We also use the Waymo Open Dataset [16] for autonomous driving in our studies. The Waymo dataset contains high-quality images taken from a camera mounted atop a vehicle to obtain real-world driving scenarios for object detection.

3.2   Evolutionary Search-Based Approach

This section describes how we harness evolutionary search to generate adversarial examples against object detection algorithms. Figure 2 shows a Data Flow Diagram (DFD) for EvoAttack, where parallel lines represent external data stores, green circles denote process bubbles, and arrows indicate data flow between processes. The inputs for the algorithm are a (black-box) object detection model and an input image (i.e., the original, non-perturbed image). The algorithm searches for perturbations that adversely impact the model's ability to detect objects. In order to apply evolutionary search, potential solutions are mapped to a genome representation in Step 1. In our work, individuals (i.e., images) are represented as 3D matrices of the following form: $[RGB\_channel, i, j]$, where each element of the matrix denotes the value of an RGB channel (ranging from [0, 255]) for the i, j-th pixel, respectively.

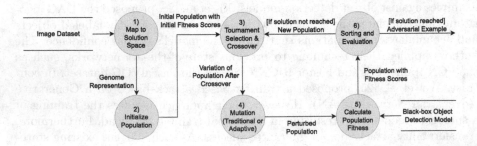

Fig. 2. DFD for the evolutionary process used to generate adversarial examples against object detection models.

We largely follow a standard generational GA process to identify adversarial examples. A point crossover operator is used in Step 3 to create children to maintain regions of perturbation that cause failures in the model's detection. Several key innovations enable EVOATTACK to optimize the evolutionary search process and reduce the perturbations in adversarial examples. First, EVOATTACK uses an adaptive mutation scheme that enables the trade-off of minimizing visible perturbation with computational time to find adversarial examples (Sect. 3.3 describes the adaptive mutation scheme in detail). Second, we introduce an optimization strategy in Step 5, where the previous generation's model results are used to configure the structure of the fitness function and identify regions of interest to perturb. The fitness scores are calculated using the following expression:

$$FitnessScore = \sum_{i=0}^{len(detection)} detection[i]['confidence']$$

The fitness score represents the model's "degree of correctness" as the sum of the confidence scores for objects identified by the model. As an object is no longer detected by the model when its confidence score is reduced below the detection threshold, the fitness score promotes the evolutionary search to introduce perturbations that iteratively lowers detection confidences until the objects are no longer detected by the model.

Finally, the population is sorted by the fitness score in Step 6. If an adversarial example is found that prevents model detection, then the algorithm terminates and returns the adversarial example. Otherwise, the new population returns to Step 3 for the algorithm to iteratively add perturbations. If the maximum number of generations is reached without convergence, then the algorithm fails and is terminated.

3.3 Adaptive Mutation Scheme

The mutation operation in Step 4 introduces perturbations to an image with the objective of finding "ideal" perturbations (i.e., fewest number of changed pixels and smallest degree of changes) that hamper model detection. The traditional approach to the mutation scheme [12,23] in evolutionary search-based attacks is to modify each pixel with a small mutation rate, P_{mut}, during the mutation step of each generation. This approach can quickly generate adversarial examples that cause a failure in the model's detection ability, where the emphasis is on optimizing computational time. However, when applied to images of large dimensions, perturbations would be introduced to many pixels even with a small mutation rate (e.g., $P_{mut} = 0.01$), thus making the attack more likely to be human perceptible. For example, an object in a bounding box of dimension 160×200 (i.e., 10% of a 640×500 image) would mutate 320 pixels on average every generation using a small P_{mut} of 0.01. After 100 generations, every pixel is expected to be mutated at least once. As such, we found that this approach would introduce perturbations to the image that are too easily perceived by humans.

In order to address the high perturbation problem, we propose an adaptive mutation scheme for EVOATTACK that begins by adding minimal perturbations and scales the added perturbations as the number of generations increases.

During the mutation step of each generation (i.e., Step 4), we introduce minor perturbations to pixels in bounding boxes identified by the model by adding perturbations sampled over $(\delta_{min}, \delta_{max})$ to n pixels for each object detected. The values $(\delta_{min}, \delta_{max})$ determine the degree of perturbation introduced. Higher δ values introduce perturbations that are more likely to cause misdetections, but are more likely to be human perceptible. The number of changed pixels n is determined by the following formula, where α, β, and P_{mut} are hyperparameters:

$$n = \begin{cases} max(\text{generation}/\alpha, 1) & \text{if generation} \leq \beta \\ \text{num\_of\_pixels} * P_{mut} * (\text{generation}/\beta) & \text{if generation} > \beta \end{cases}$$

Specifically, n is increased incrementally every α number of generations. The value α determines the rate of growth for the number of pixels perturbed. The value β defines the number of generations EVOATTACK explores before the algorithm adopts a more aggressive search strategy to promote convergence. After β number of generations, n is instead based on the number of pixels in the bounding box multiplied by a mutation rate (i.e., P_{mut}) that increases dynamically based on the generation count. For example, consider the object in an image discussed above with dimension 160×200 and $\alpha = 15, \beta = 750, P_{mut} = 0.01$. EVOATTACK introduces perturbations to each detected object that incrementally increase by 1 every 15 generations (i.e., 1 pixel is changed from generations 1–15, 2 pixels are changed from generations 15–30, etc.) until the 750th generation. By the 750th generation, 320 pixels in the bounding box of each object are mutated. The algorithm then modifies a number of pixels based on a scaling mutation rate, P_{mut}. Using an adaptive mutation scheme, images that do not require large perturbations to cause a misdetection will not have unnecessary perturbations, while images that are difficult to perturb will still be promoted to converge as the number of generations increases.

4   Empirical Studies

We evaluate the efficacy of EVOATTACK against state-of-the-art object detection algorithms. First, we demonstrate that the adaptive mutation scheme can generate more adverse test data (less perturbations) than the traditional mutation scheme (i.e., all pixels in bounding boxes are eligible for mutation with a fixed chance). Second, we show that our approach is model agnostic by attacking models of different architectures. Finally, we demonstrate the potential negative impacts of such attacks by attacking the Waymo Open Dataset [16], while also demonstrating that it is data agnostic.

4.1   Experimental Setup for Evolutionary Search-Based Approaches

For the validation work, we use object detection DNNs implemented using the Pytorch [15] deep learning research platform. To show that our attack is model agnostic, we use various model architectures with weights pretrained by Pytorch, such as a Faster R-CNN MobileNetV3 [20] and RetinaNet [10] trained using a ResNet-50-FPN backbone. For Waymo images, we train an object detector using a RetinaNet with a ResNet-50-FPN backbone [8]. The trained model has a mean recall of 95%. During model inference, we set the detection confidence threshold to be 0.7 to provide a proof-of-concept demonstration of EvoAttack. However, EvoAttack can generate adversarial examples using any threshold score for model testing. For evolutionary parameters, we started with values used in state-of-the-art image classification attacks [12,23]. We experimentally fine-tuned these parameters for object detection. The maximum number of generations is set to 2000, with 16 individuals in each population. Finally, $P_{crossover}$ and P_{mut} are set to 0.6 and 0.01, respectively. In order to provide a baseline comparison for EvoAttack, we have implemented a random search algorithm that iteratively adds perturbations to a random number of pixels each generation. The random search is not population based and does not use any evolutionary operators other than random mutation. Finally, since EvoAttack is intended to be used as a testing technique before the model is deployed, we use the objective of minimizing perturbations as the primary metric to gauge attack efficiency in order to obtain higher quality adversarial examples (i.e., less perturbation) over quantity (i.e., time). Additionally, the number of generations cannot be used to adequately compare adversarial examples, as each algorithm adds a different amount of perturbation to the image per generation. All experiments are performed on a NVIDIA GeForce GTX 1080 GPU with an Intel Core i7-7700K CPU.

4.2   E1: Demonstration of the Adaptive Mutation Operator

In our first experiment, we demonstrate how adversarial examples can be generated against object detection algorithms using EvoAttack. Specifically, we illustrate the notable impact of EvoAttack's adaptive mutation scheme by including a comparison for adversarial examples generated with random search, EvoAttack using the traditional mutation scheme (denoted as EvoAttack.Trad), and EvoAttack using the adaptive mutation scheme (denoted as EvoAttack). During each mutation operation after crossover, we introduce minor perturbations to pixels in the bounding boxes identified by the object detection model in the previous generation. If a pixel is chosen for mutation, then perturbations sampled over a uniform distribution between $(\delta_{min}, \delta_{max})$ are introduced to each RGB channel of the pixel. For experiment E1, we used $\delta_{min} = 0.025$ and $\delta_{max} = 0.05$. Values for α and β are selected empirically based on from multiple runs of the experiment on the COCO dataset.

Figure 3 shows two adversarial examples generated over a randomly sampled set of input images obtained from the COCO testset against the RetinaNet model. The first image shows the model's output on the clean input image. Bounding boxes are drawn and labeled over objects identified with a confidence score of ≥ 0.7. Next, the noise filters show the differences between the original input and the adversarial examples, amplified by a factor of 10 for readability. The adversarial examples in the rightmost column of images prevent model detection, where the model failed to draw bounding boxes around the objects of interest. The adversarial examples shown on top and bottom are generated using EVOATTACK.TRAD and EVOATTACK, respectively. The perturbation information shows the number of generations required for convergence, number of changed pixels (L0 norm), and degree of perturbations (L2 norm or Euclidean distance) of the adversarial examples. The numbers in parenthesis denote the percentage of pixels in the original bounding boxes that have been modified in the adversarial example. Figure 3a shows a scene at a skateboarding event. The model identified multiple objects of interest in the image and drew bounding boxes around them. Both mutation schemes generated an adversarial example that caused the model to fail to detect the objects. Compared to the adversarial example generated by EVOATTACK.TRAD, the adversarial example generated by EVOATTACK contains significantly fewer perturbations. Since EVOATTACK converged on an adversarial example before the β number of generations, the adversarial example is considered to be "easy to perturb". In contrast, Fig. 3b shows an input image of a skier. The adversarial examples generated also caused a failure in the model's detection. However, compared to Fig. 3a, this input image required more than β number of generations to converge, thus EVOATTACK only slightly outperforms EVOATTACK.TRAD in minimizing perturbations.

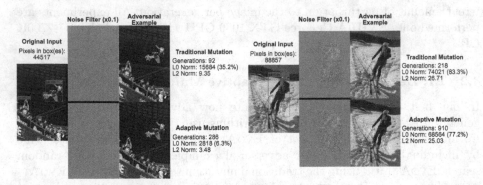

(a) Example of an easy to perturb image   (b) Example of a difficult to perturb image

Fig. 3. Comparisons of adversarial examples generated using EVOATTACK and EVOAT-TACK.TRAD. The original predicted inputs, noise filters, adversarial examples, and perturbation information are shown for each image.

Table 1 shows the average number of changed pixels and degree of perturbations for adversarial examples generated against thirty randomly sampled input images. Using traditional mutation and adaptive mutation, EVOATTACK performs better than random search. In Table 1, the percentage of pixels in bounding boxes changed metric for random search exceeds 100%, since the algorithm perturbs a random number of pixels in the entire image (i.e., modifies pixels beyond the bounding boxes and does not localize the perturbation). With the adaptive mutation scheme, EVOATTACK has fewer perturbations when compared to EVOATTACK.TRAD that uses traditional mutation. Specifically, 26 adversarial examples generated with EVOATTACK have fewer number of changed pixels and 19 adversarial examples generated have less degree of perturbations when compared to EVOATTACK.TRAD. The average number of changed pixels is reduced by 31.41% and the average degree of perturbations is reduced by 21.49% using EVOATTACK. The columns labeled *"Easy to perturb inputs"* show the measured metrics for adversarial examples that are perturbed before β number of generations in EVOATTACK. The metrics for the same set of images for EVOATTACK.TRAD are also provided for comparison. The results indicate that EVOATTACK is able to find adversarial examples with significantly less perturbations for objects that are easy to perturb, with 81.96% reduced number of changed pixels and 64.67% reduced degree of perturbations on average. The results of this experiment show that EVOATTACK is able to generate adversarial examples with low degree of perturbations and few number of pixel changes.

Table 1. Comparison of perturbations measured for adversarial examples generated over thirty input images against a RetinaNet model. The easy to perturb inputs consist of images that converged before β number of generations in EVOATTACK. The metrics for the same set of images from an evolutionary search using the traditional mutation scheme are provided for comparison.

Avg. Statistic		All Inputs		Easy to Perturb Inputs	
Num of objects in input		2.73		2.55	
Num of pixels in bnd. boxes		114,670		92,332	
Total number of images		30		20	
Avg. Values (per image)	Random	EvoAttack (Trad.)	EvoAttack (Adapt.)	EvoAttack (Trad.)	EvoAttack (Adapt.)
Num of generations	71.37	231.07	625.50	130.50	376.90
Num of changed pixels	277,955.94	59,430.57	40,762.67	33,916.95	6,119.35
% of pixels in bnd. boxes changed	242.37%	51.83%	35.55%	36.73%	6.63%
Degree of perturbations	337.33	22.33	17.53	14.04	4.96
Computational time (sec)	813.11	677.91	1,496.31	329.19	768.47

4.3 E2: Demonstration that EvoAttack is Model Agnostic

In this experiment, we demonstrate that EVOATTACK is model agnostic by attacking a model of different architecture. Specifically, we apply EVOATTACK to a Faster R-CNN MobileNetV3 [20] model and show that we can produce comparable results as an attack against the RetinaNet [10]. Against the same set of thirty input images, our approach is able to reduce all detected objects below the detection threshold. Table 2 shows the average perturbations of adversarial examples generated against the Faster R-CNN model.

Compared to the RetinaNet model, the Faster R-CNN model is more robust on average against EVOATTACK, as it requires more perturbations to prevent model detection. In our studies, we found that the Faster R-CNN model requires almost twice the number of changed pixels and degree of perturbations when compared to the RetinaNet model. Furthermore, the number of adversarial examples that were generated before the β number of generations reduced significantly from 20 to 6 for the Faster R-CNN using EVOATTACK, implying that there are fewer images that require low perturbations to cause a misdetection. Thus, this experiment shows that EVOATTACK is model agnostic and demonstrates EVOATTACK as a testing technique to determine that the Faster R-CNN model is more robust than the RetinaNet model.

Table 2. Comparison of perturbations measured for adversarial examples generated over thirty input images against a Faster R-CNN model.

Avg. Statistic	All Inputs		Easy to Perturb Inputs	
Num of objects in input	2.93		1.67	
Num of pixels in bnd. boxes	146,338		58,428	
Total number of images	30		6	

Avg. Values (per image)	Random	EvoAttack (Trad.)	EvoAttack (Adapt.)	EvoAttack (Trad.)	EvoAttack (Adapt.)
Num of generations	89.77	509.33	988.73	80.00	435.67
Num of changed pixels	280,679.41	110,466.38	101,815.88	27,136.17	6,410.50
% of pixels in bnd. box changed	191.8%	75.49%	69.58%	46.44%	10.97%
Degree of perturbations	414.45	41.06	39.91	12.36	5.29
Computational time (sec)	862.85	1,008.77	1,145.01	90.96	181.13

4.4   E3: Demonstration that EvoAttack is Data Agnostic

The purpose of this experiment is to demonstrate that EVOATTACK is data agnostic and illustrate the potential impact of such attacks on real-world scenarios (e.g., contexts relevant to autonomous vehicles). We apply EVOATTACK to a RetinaNet [8] trained over the Waymo Open Dataset [16]. The trained model predicts vehicles, pedestrians, and cyclists for a camera mounted atop a vehicle. Thus, if an adversary successfully prevents correct model detection, the resulting behavior of the system may lead to significant consequences such as serious injuries or even deaths. We apply EVOATTACK to thirty randomly chosen images sampled over the Waymo Open Dataset. Figure 4 shows several adversarial examples. This result shows that our approach successfully introduced perturbations such that the model fails to draw correct bounding boxes around vehicles, pedestrians, and cyclists in the images. We also show the potential impact of black-box adversarial attacks on real-world safety-critical systems. If an object detection model used in an autonomous vehicle is compromised using such attacks, then the behavior of the vehicle may result in a collision with surrounding vehicles or people.

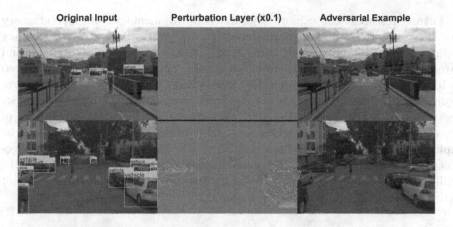

Fig. 4. Adversarial examples generated against the Waymo Open Dataset [16].

4.5 Threats to Validity

The results in this paper are limited to adversarial examples generated using evolutionary search on DNNs for object detection algorithms. The results of the experiments may vary with each run, as evolutionary search-based algorithms rely on non-determinism to evolve solutions. To ensure the feasibility of the approach, a wide variety of randomly sampled images were chosen. Additionally, the measured Coefficient of Variation (CV) for a wide variety of inputs and models over multiple repetitions of the experiments of EVOATTACK are all less than 0.15, indicating that multiple runs of EVOATTACK on the same image produce adversarial examples with similar and comparable degree of perturbations and number of generations. For random search, a high variance is measured in repeated experiments due to the broad variation in the number of pixels changed. However, the perturbations (i.e., L0 and L2 norms) of the best performing adversarial examples of the repeated random searches are still significantly worse than EVOATTACK's adversarial examples. The images selected as examples for display are also chosen randomly. There is no post-selection process applied.

5 Conclusion

This paper introduced EVOATTACK, an evolutionary search-based attack to generate adversarial examples against object detection algorithms. We showed that our approach can attack object detection algorithms without having access to model parameters, architecture, or estimates of the gradient. The search-based process uses the results of previous iterations of the evolutionary process to configure the structure of the fitness function and guide the mutation process. Furthermore, we introduced an adaptive mutation scheme that reduces both the number of perturbations and the degree of change for object detection adversarial examples. We conducted a series of experiments to show how adversarial examples can be generated against images from various datasets and models of various architectures.

Future research will explore potential improvements to our evolutionary search-based attack and explore detection and mitigation strategies. They include potential improvements using multi-objective GAs (e.g., NSGA-II) and parallel GAs. Various hyperparameter tuning approaches may be explored to identify optimal hyperparameters for EVOATTACK. We will also perform more empirical studies to compare the effectiveness of EVOATTACK with existing white-box attacks. Additionally, research to improve the robustness of object detection models through adversarial training with EVOATTACK will be explored. Furthermore, novelty search [7,9] may be leveraged to discover a collection of adversarial examples that causes diverse behaviors in the model. Finally, Enlil [8] (i.e., behavior oracles) may be used to predict the uncertain behavior of the object detection model when exposed to adversarial examples.

References

1. Carlini, N., Wagner, D.: Towards evaluating the robustness of neural networks. In: 2017 IEEE Symposium on Security and Privacy (SP), pp. 39–57. IEEE (2017)
2. Chen, J., Su, M., Shen, S., Xiong, H., Zheng, H.: POBA-GA: perturbation optimized black-box adversarial attacks via genetic algorithm. Comput. Secur. **85**, 89–106 (2019)
3. Goodfellow, I., Shlens, J., Szegedy, C.: Explaining and harnessing adversarial examples. In: International Conference on Learning Representations (2015)
4. Han, J.K., Kim, H., Woo, S.S.: Nickel to LEGO: using Foolgle to create adversarial examples to fool Google cloud speech-to-text API. In: Proceedings of the 2019 ACM SIGSAC Conference on Computer and Communications Security, CCS 2019, pp. 2593–2595. Association for Computing Machinery, New York (2019)
5. Knight, J.C.: Safety critical systems: challenges and directions. In: Proceedings of the 24th International Conference on Software Engineering, ICSE 2002, pp. 547–550 (2002)
6. Kocić, J., Jovičić, N., Drndarević, V.: An end-to-end deep neural network for autonomous driving designed for embedded automotive platforms. Sensors **19**(9), 2064 (2019)
7. Langford, M.A., Cheng, B.H.C.: Enki: a diversity-driven approach to test and train robust learning-enabled systems. ACM Trans. Auton. Adapt. Syst. (TAAS) **15**(2), 1–32 (2021)
8. Langford, M.A., Cheng, B.H.C.: "Know what you know": predicting behavior for learning-enabled systems when facing uncertainty. In: 2021 International Symposium on Software Engineering for Adaptive and Self-Managing Systems (SEAMS), pp. 78–89 (2021)
9. Lehman, J., Stanley, K.O.: Abandoning objectives: evolution through the search for novelty alone. Evol. Comput. **19**(2), 189–223 (2011)
10. Lin, T.Y., Goyal, P., Girshick, R., He, K., Dollár, P.: Focal loss for dense object detection. In: Proceedings of the IEEE International Conference on Computer Vision, pp. 2980–2988 (2017)
11. Marie-Sainte, S.L., Alamir, M.B., Alsaleh, D., Albakri, G., Zouhair, J.: Enhancing credit card fraud detection using deep neural network. In: Arai, K., Kapoor, S., Bhatia, R. (eds.) SAI 2020. AISC, vol. 1229, pp. 301–313. Springer, Cham (2020). https://doi.org/10.1007/978-3-030-52246-9_21

12. Alzantot, M., et al.: GenAttack: practical black-box attacks with gradient-free optimization. In: Proceedings of the Genetic and Evolutionary Computation Conference, pp. 1111–1119 (2019)
13. Eykholt, K., et al.: Robust physical-world attacks on deep learning visual classification. In: Proceedings of the IEEE Conference on Computer Vision and Pattern Recognition, pp. 1625–1634 (2018)
14. Lin, T.Y., et al.: Microsoft COCO: common objects in context. In: Fleet, D., Pajdla, T., Schiele, B., Tuytelaars, T. (eds.) ECCV 2014. LNCS, vol. 8693, pp. 740–755. Springer, Cham (2014). https://doi.org/10.1007/978-3-319-10602-1_48
15. Paszke, A., et al.: PyTorch: an imperative style, high-performance deep learning library. In: Wallach, H., Larochelle, H., Beygelzimer, A., d'Alché-Buc, F., Fox, E., Garnett, R. (eds.) Advances in Neural Information Processing Systems, vol. 32, pp. 8024–8035. Curran Associates, Inc. (2019)
16. Sun, P., et al.: Scalability in perception for autonomous driving: Waymo open dataset. In: Proceedings of the IEEE/CVF Conference on Computer Vision and Pattern Recognition, pp. 2446–2454 (2020)
17. Szegedy, C., et al.: Intriguing properties of neural networks. In: International Conference on Learning Representations (2014)
18. Moosavi-Dezfooli, S.M., Fawzi, A., Frossard, P.: DeepFool: a simple and accurate method to fool deep neural networks. In: Proceedings of the IEEE Conference on Computer Vision and Pattern Recognition, pp. 2574–2582 (2016)
19. Nandita, G., Chandra, T.M.: Malicious host detection and classification in cloud forensics with DNN and SFLO approaches. Int. J. Syst. Assur. Eng. Manag. 1–13 (2021). https://doi.org/10.1007/s13198-021-01168-x
20. Ren, S., He, K., Girshick, R., Sun, J.: Faster R-CNN: towards real-time object detection with region proposal networks. In: Advances in Neural Information Processing Systems, vol. 28 (2015)
21. Rudd, E.M., Harang, R., Saxe, J.: MEADE: towards a malicious email attachment detection engine. In: 2018 IEEE International Symposium on Technologies for Homeland Security (HST), pp. 1–7 (2018)
22. Su, J., Vargas, D.V., Sakurai, K.: One pixel attack for fooling deep neural networks. IEEE Trans. Evol. Comput. 23(5), 828–841 (2019)
23. Vidnerová, P., Neruda, R.: Vulnerability of classifiers to evolutionary generated adversarial examples. Neural Netw. 127, 168–181 (2020)
24. Wang, Y., Xu, W.: Leveraging deep learning with LDA-based text analytics to detect automobile insurance fraud. Decis. Support Syst. 105, 87–95 (2018)
25. Wei, X., Liang, S., Chen, N., Cao, X.: Transferable adversarial attacks for image and video object detection. In: Proceedings of the 28th International Joint Conference on Artificial Intelligence, IJCAI 2019, pp. 954–960. AAAI Press (2019)
26. Wu, B., Iandola, F., Jin, P.H., Keutzer, K.: SqueezeDet: unified, small, low power fully convolutional neural networks for real-time object detection for autonomous driving. In: Proceedings of the IEEE Conference on Computer Vision and Pattern Recognition Workshops, pp. 129–137 (2017)
27. Wu, C., Luo, W., Zhou, N., Xu, P., Zhu, T.: Genetic algorithm with multiple fitness functions for generating adversarial examples. In: 2021 IEEE Congress on Evolutionary Computation (CEC), pp. 1792–1799 (2021)
28. Xie, C., Wang, J., Zhang, Z., Zhou, Y., Xie, L., Yuille, A.: Adversarial examples for semantic segmentation and object detection. In: Proceedings of the IEEE International Conference on Computer Vision, pp. 1369–1378 (2017)
29. Yuan, X., He, P., Zhu, Q., Li, X.: Adversarial examples: attacks and defenses for deep learning. IEEE Trans. Neural Netw. Learn. Syst. 30(9), 2805–2824 (2019)

NIER and RENE Tracks

Applying Combinatorial Testing
to Verification-Based Fairness Testing

Takashi Kitamura[2]([⊠]) [iD], Zhenjiang Zhao[1][iD], and Takahisa Toda[1][iD]

[1] National Institute of Advanced Industrial Science and Technology (AIST),
Tokyo, Japan
t.kitamura@aist.go.jp
[2] Graduate School of Informatics and Engineering,
University of Electro-Communications, Tokyo, Japan
{zhenjiang,toda}@disc.lab.uec.ac.jp

Abstract. Fairness testing, given a machine learning classifier, detects discriminatory data contained in it via executing test cases. In this paper, we propose a new approach to fairness testing named VBT-CT, which applies combinatorial t-way testing (CT) to Verification Based Testing (VBT) VDT is a state-of-the-art fairness testing method, which represents a given classifier under test in logical constraints and searches for test cases by solving such constraints. CT is a coverage-based sampling technique, with an ability to sample diverse test data from a search space specified by logical constraints. We implement a proof-of-concept of VBT-CT, and see its feasibility by experiments. We also discuss its advantages, current limitations, and further research directions.

Keywords: Fairness testing · Combinatorial interaction testing · Testing machine learning

1 Introduction

Algorithm fairness refers to a property of machine learning (ML) algorithms that such ML algorithms (a. k. a., classifiers) make discriminatory decisions with respect to sensitive attributes, e.g., gender, race, age, etc. According to wider adoption of ML-based decision making algorithms in our daily life, the concern on algorithm fairness is growing. For example, COMPAS algorithm, which predicts future criminals of defendants, used to determine criminal sentencing, is known to be biased against black defendants [4].

Individual fairness (IF) [2] is a central concept of ML algorithm fairness, which refers to that an ML classifier should give similar decisions to similar individuals but differ in sensitive attributes. For example, consider an ML classifier LOAN, which assesses the creditworthiness of loan applicants (i.e., individuals). Individuals are here schemed by the three attributes of 'gender', 'income', and 'age', exemplified by the following two data instances:

$$x1 :(gender = male, \quad income = 1000, age = 40) \qquad (1)$$
$$x2 :(gender = female, income = 1000, age = 40), \qquad (2)$$

M. Papadakis and S. R. Vergilio (Eds.): SSBSE 2022, LNCS 13711, pp. 101–107, 2022.
https://doi.org/10.1007/978-3-031-21251-2_7

and we set 'gender' as the sensitive attribute. Note that the two individuals are similar, as they are identical except for the sensitive attribute. Suppose now that the classifier LOAN gives different decision to the two similar individuals, e.g., '1 (Yes)' to x_1 and '0 (No)' to x_2. We say x_1 (and x_2) violates IF, and call such data instances *discriminatory data*.

Testing is an approach to the IF concern, first addressed by Galhotra et al. [3]. Its main functionality is, given a classifier under test (CUT), to detect discriminatory data contained the given CUT. A number of testing techniques for IF have been proposed so far, e.g., [3,8–12,14]. While such IF testing techniques differ in technical details, their common characteristic as testing techniques is to detect discriminatory data by generating test cases and running them against the CUT. The key challenge of IF testing is thus on a search problem of how to efficiently generate (or, search) a limited number of effective test cases, from the huge input space of the CUT.

In this paper, we propose an idea on a new approach to IF testing, named VBT-CT, which applies combinatorial t-way testing (CT) [6] to Verification Based Testing (VBT) [11]. VBT is a state-of-the-art black-box IF testing technique. It represents a given CUT in logical constraints and searches for test cases by solving such constraints. Combinatorial t-way testing (CT) is a coverage-based data sampling technique, which can sample diverse data sets, equipped with the ability to flexibly specify the sampling space by logical constraints. Our idea is that by applying CT in the test search part of VBT, VBT-CT can enhance the ability of detecting discriminatory data of VBT. We implement a proof-of-concept of VBT-CT, and see its feasibility by experiments. We also discuss its advantages, current limitations, and further research directions.

2   Preliminary

This section briefly reviews Verification Based Testing (VBT) [11] and Combinatorial t-way testing (CT) [6].

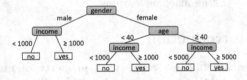

Fig. 1. A decision tree for predicting who gets a loan

2.1   Verification Based Testing

Figure 2 shows the overview of VBT. VBT takes a classifier under test (CUT) as input, and outputs individual discriminatory data instances contained in the CUT. The mechanism of VBT iterates over the following steps: At the first step, VBT constructs approximation classifier of the given CUT, by training a decision tree (DT) with the a training data set made using the CUT. Second, VBT encodes the DT into SMT constraints. The third step is test generation, where VBT searches for test cases using SMT solving (using Z3) to the constraints amalgamating the constraints for (1) the SMT-represented decision tree, (2) individual fairness, and (3) sampling strategies. The generated test cases are executed against the CUT, to check if a test case is actually a discriminatory data

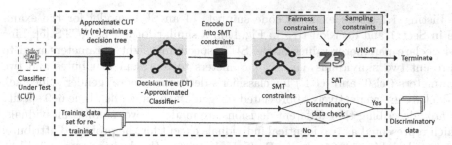

Fig. 2. Verification based testing

instance in the CUT. Passing test cases are collected as detected discriminatory data, and failing ones are used for training data for re-training the approximation classifier for the next iteration.

A key challenge in VBT is on test generation part for how to efficiently search for effective test cases. Sampling strategies here play an important role. Two strategies are proposed for the sampling constraints, (a. k. a., search strategies): *data pruning* and *brunch pruning*. The brunch pruning, which it is reported performs better [11], searches for test cases by traversing the decision trees, aiming to diversify generated test cases.

2.2 Combinatorial *t*-Way Testing (CT)

Combinatorial *t*-way testing (CT) is a data sampling technique [6] from sampling spaces specified by logical constraints. CT presumes a system under test (SUT) model, to specify input space of SUT, consisting of two description components: (1) *parameter-values*, the list of parameters and their values of the SUT and (2) *logical constraints*, which specify the shape of input space by logical relation over parameter-values. The *t*-way coverage criterion of CT, given the strength $t \in \mathbb{N}$, stipulates to cover all valid value combinations of size t (a. k. a., *t*-way tuples) of the SUT model, where we say that a value combination is *valid* if it complies with the constraints. A test set that satisfies the *t*-way coverage criterion is called a *t-way test set*. A number of CT generation algorithm have been proposed, and some implemented tools are publicly available e.g., ACTS [5], PICT [7].

3 Proposed Approach: VBT-CT

VBT-CT uses CT test generation in the test generation part of VBT. Our implementation to this is to make an SUT model for CT from the given decision tree, and apply a CT algorithm to it. For the parameter-value list part of the SUT model, we prepare a pair of parameters for each attribute (such as, 'gender', 'race', 'income') and parameters for classifier's decisions, to represent two individuals. For the constraint part, two constraint blocks are specified to represent fairness and decision trees, respectively noted *Unfair* and *DecTree*.

Listing 1.1 shows example code snippets of an SUT model for the example in Sect. 1 and decision tree in Fig. 1, in a similar format as ACTS [5]. Line 1–4 declare parameter-values of the SUT, specifying eight parameters used to represent two individuals, i.e., six parameters to represent attributes and two parameters ('cls0' and 'cls1') for classifier's decisions, where 'gender', 'income', and 'class' are respectively abbreviated by 'gen', 'age', and 'cls'. Line 6–9 specify *Unfair*, describing that different decisions are made to two 'similar' individuals, which represented as two identical individuals except for the protected attribute, i.e., 'gender'. Line 11–21 specify *DecTree*, describing the decision tree in Table 2. Table 1 shows a 3-way test set of the SUT model in Listing 1.1. Each row represents a test case, i.e., the test set contains six test cases.

```
1 [Parameter]
2 gen0(enum): m,f; age0(int): 10,20,30,40,50,60; inc0(int):50,1000,3000,5000
3 gen1(enum): m,f; age1(int): 10,20,30,40,50,60; inc1(int):50,1000,3000,5000
4 cls0(int): 0,1; cls1 (int): 0,1
5 [Constraint]
6 -- Unfair
7 (gen0=m && gen1=f)  || (gen0=f && gen1=m)
8 (age0=1 && age1=1)  || (age0=2 && age1=2)|| ... || (age0=6 && age1=6)
9 (inc0=50 && inc1=50)||(inc0=1000 && inc1=1000)|| ... (inc0=5000 && inc1
      =5000)
10 (cls0=0 && cls1=1)
11 -- Decision Tree
12 (gen0=m && inc0<1000) => cls0=0; (gen0=m && inc0>=1000) => cls1=0
13 (gen0=f && age0<40 && inc0<1000) => cls0=0
14 (gen0=f && age0<40) && inc0>= 1000) => cls0=0
15 (gen0=f && age0>=40) && inc0< 5000) => cls0=0
16 (gen0=f && age0>=40) && inc0>= 5000) => cls0=0
17 (gen1=m && inc1<1000) => cls1=0; (gen1=m && inc1>=1000) => cls1=1
18 (gen1=f && age1<40) && inc1< 1000) => cls1=0
19 (gen1=f && age1<40) && inc1>= 1000) => cls1=1
20 (gen1=f && age1>=40) && inc1< 5000) => cls1=0
21 (gen1=f && age1>=40) && inc1>=5000) => cls1=1
```

Listing 1.1. Code snippets of an SUT model in a similar format to ACTS [5]

4 Experiments

We conduct small experiments to confirm the feasibility of VBT-CT. We implemented a proof-of-concept of the proposed idea (i.e., VBT-CT), by modifying the code of VBT by [11]. For experiments, we use Census Income dataset[1], and four classifiers, which are Logistic Regression (LR), Random Forest (RF), Naive Bayes (NB), Decision Tree (DT), and set 'gender' and 'race' as the protected attribute. We run VBT-CT until 200 test cases are generated, in comparison with VBT. For each configuration, we execute 3 trials and take the average of them. Intel(R) Xeon(R) Silver 4210 CPU @ 2.20 GHz Processor, 32 GB memory, running Ubuntu 20.04.4 LTS.

Table 1. A 3-way test set of SUT model of Listing 1.1

No.	gen0	gen1	age0	age1	inc0	inc1	cls0	cls1
1	f	m	40	40	1000	1000	0	1
2	f	m	40	40	3000	3000	0	1
3	f	m	50	50	1000	1000	0	1
4	f	m	50	50	3000	3000	0	1
5	f	m	60	60	1000	1000	0	1
6	f	m	60	60	3000	3000	0	1

---

[1] https://archive.ics.uci.edu/ml/datasets/adult.

Table 2. Summary of experiments. Columns for '#Disc', 'Prec.' and Time (s)' respectively show the numbers of detected discriminatory data, precision (i.e., hit ratio of # of discriminatory data over # of generated test cases), and execution times (in seconds) of VBT and VBT-CT, for configurations given in rows. ▲ means dis-improvement ratio.

No.	Clf.	Prot. attribute	VBT			VBT-CT			Improvement ratio		
			#Disc	Prec.	Time(s)	#Disc	Prec.	Time(s)	#Disc	Prec.	Time
1	LR	Gender	5.0	**0.063**	**18.8**	**8.3**	0.060	44388.2	1.67	0.95	▲2361.1
2	LR	Race	5.3	0.027	**32.0**	**8.0**	**0.040**	14213.0	1.50	1.50	▲444.2
3	RF	Gender	52.7	0.263	**47.0**	**58.7**	**0.293**	250312.1	1.11	1.11	▲5325.8
4	RF	Race	**3.3**	**0.017**	**51.3**		time out		N/A	N/A	N/A
5	NB	Gender	53.7	0.268	**26.3**	**129.0**	**0.645**	488.8	2.40	2.40	▲18.6
6	NB	Race	9.3	0.047	**25.3**	**75.3**	**0.377**	3323.3	8.07	8.07	▲125.4
7	DT	Gender	100.7	0.503	**32.1**	**144.0**	**0.720**	143204.2	1.43	1.43	▲4461.2
8	DT	Race	**147.3**	**0.737**	**32.8**	134.7	0.673	99241.8	0.91	0.91	▲3025.7
		avg./total	377.3	0.24	267.5	558.0	0.35	555171.5	1.47	1.46	▲2251.7
		#wins	2	3	8	6	5	0			

Table 2 shows the results of experiments. The results suggest that VBT-CT more effectively detects discriminatory data than VBT, since it detects more discriminatory data six out of eight configurations and 1.47 times in average. We can also observe superiority of VBT-CT on precision. On the other hand, VBT-CT runs slower than VBT by 2251.7 times in average. This is an obvious limitation that VBT-CT needs to overcome. Recall, however, that the current implementation of VBT-CT is given in the most naive way, as this paper focuses on reporting feasibility aspect of VBT-CT at this research phase.

5   Related Work

Testing IF is an active research subject, and various techniques have been proposed such as THEMIS [3], AEQUITAS [12], SG [1], ADF [14], CGFT [8,9], in addition to VBT [10]. Among such study, CGFT [8] and the technique by Patel et al. [9] have attempted to apply CT to IF testing.

CGFT [8] applies CT to AEQUITAS [12], another IF testing technique, to improve its testing ability. As the search algorithm of AEQUITAS is structured with several phases, CGFT applies CT to the search phase called *global search*, replacing a random search. The global search of AEQUITAS (and thus CGFT) searches for test cases from the input space of CUT (similarly to VBT-CT), however, CGFT does not make any use of constraints of CT in doing so. As a possible limitation, this approach may surfer from low precision that generated test cases detect discriminatory data, since it cannot employ any guides in searching the input space for test cases, while VBT-CT can do so using approximation classifiers.

The technique by Patel et al. [9] combines CT and a Explainable Artificial Intelligence (XAI) technique, where CT is used in the phase to search for test cases from the input space of CUT. It makes use of constraints in doing so, where it applies an association rule mining to training datasets to retrieve constraints.

We plan comparison of the constraint retrieval techniques between VBT-CT and the technique by Patel et al. is a direction of further work of VBT-CT.

6   Discussion and Future Work

We propose a new approach to IF testing, named VBT-CT, which applies CT to VBT [11], an IF testing technique by Sharma and Wehrheim. We implemented a proof-concept of VBT-CT, and demonstrate its feasibility by preliminary experiments. We also discuss its advantages and current limitations.

There are many directions for further work, including the following: The first direction is to tackle the limitation on efficiency of the current implementation of VBT-CT. A possible solution is to use a CT algorithm that are designed to efficiently handle complex logical constraints (such as, [13]^2), in place of ACTS used in VBT-CT. A more promising approach would be to develop a CT algorithm dedicated for the test generation used in VBT-CT, by leveraging the fact that the logical constraints of SUT models handled in VBT-CT are specific to *Unfair* and *DecTree*. Third, we are also interested in applying the proposed approach to MLCHECK[10], which extends VBT with the use of deep neural network (DNN) for the approximation classifier, instead of decision tree.

Acknowledgements. This paper is partly based on results obtained from a project, JPNP20006, commissioned by the New Energy and Industrial Technology Development Organization (NEDO).

References

1. Aggarwal, A., Lohia, P., Nagar, S., Dey, K., Saha, D.: Black box fairness testing of machine learning models. In: Proceedings of ESEC/SIGSOFT FSE, pp. 625–635 (2019). https://doi.org/10.1145/3338906.3338937
2. Dwork, C., Hardt, M., Pitassi, T., Reingold, O., Zemel, R.: Fairness through awareness. In: Proceedings of ITCS 2012, pp. 214–226 (2012)
3. Galhotra, S., Brun, Y., Meliou, A.: Fairness testing: testing software for discrimination. In: Proceedings of ESEC/FSE 2017, pp. 498–510. ACM (2017)
4. Angwin, J., Larson, J., Mattu, S., Kirchner, L.: Machine bias (2016). https://www.propublica.org/article/machine-bias-risk-assessments-in-criminal-sentencing
5. Kuhn, R.: Automated combinatorial testing for software (2016). https://csrc.nist.gov/projects/automated-combinatorial-testing-for-software. Accessed 24 Feb 2021
6. Kuhn, R., Kacker, R.: Introduction to Combinatorial Testing. Chapman & Hall CRC (2013)
7. Microsoft: Pairwise independent combinatorial testing. https://github.com/microsoft/pict
8. Morales, D.P., Kitamura, T., Takada, S.: Coverage-guided fairness testing. In: Proceedings of ICIS 2021, pp. 183–199 (2021)
9. Patel, A.R., Chandrasekaran, J., Lei, Y., Kacker, R.N., Kuhn, D.R.: A combinatorial approach to fairness testing of machine learning models. In: Proceedings of IWCT 2022, pp. 1135–1144. IEEE (2022)

---

^{2} We do not find their algorithm implementation is publicly available.

10. Sharma, A., Demir, C., Ngomo, A.N., Wehrheim, H.: MLCHECK-property-driven testing of machine learning classifiers. In: Proceedings of ICMLA 2021, pp. 738–745. IEEE (2021)
11. Sharma, A., Wehrheim, H.: Automatic fairness testing of machine learning models. In: Casola, V., De Benedictis, A., Rak, M. (eds.) ICTSS 2020. LNCS, vol. 12543, pp. 255–271. Springer, Cham (2020). https://doi.org/10.1007/978-3-030-64881-7_16
12. Udeshi, S., Arora, P., Chattopadhyay, S.: Automated directed fairness testing. In: Proceedings of ASE 2018, pp. 98–108 (2018)
13. Yamada, A., Biere, A., Artho, C., Kitamura, T., Choi, E.: Greedy combinatorial test case generation using unsatisfiable cores. In: Proceedings of ASE 2016, pp. 614–624. ACM (2016)
14. Zhang, P., et al.: White-box fairness testing through adversarial sampling. In: Proceedings of ICSE 2020, pp. 949–960. ACM (2020)

Challenge Track

Multi-objective Genetic Improvement: A Case Study with EvoSuite

James Callan[✉] and Justyna Petke

University College London, London, UK
{james.callan.19,j.petke}@ucl.ac.uk

Abstract. Automated multi-objective software optimisation offers an attractive solution to software developers wanting to balance often conflicting objectives, such as memory consumption and execution time. Work on using multi-objective search-based approaches to optimise for such non-functional software behaviour has so far been scarce, with tooling unavailable for use. To fill this gap we extended an existing generalist, open source, genetic improvement tool, Gin, with a multi-objective search strategy, NSGA-II. We ran our implementation on a mature, large software to show its use. In particular, we chose EvoSuite—a tool for automatic test case generation for Java. We use our multi-objective extension of Gin to improve both the execution time and memory usage of EvoSuite. We find improvements to execution time of up to 77.8% and improvements to memory of up to 9.2% on our test set. We also release our code, providing the first open source multi-objective genetic improvement tooling for improvement of memory and runtime for Java.

Keywords: Genetic improvement · Multi-objective optimisation · Search-based software engineering

1 Introduction

Performance is one of the key properties of software. Programs that are laggy, consume a lot of resources, are not only a source of user complaints, but can render such software unsustainable and unusable. Even though there have been extensive studies on software performance issues, e.g., [9], and tools have been proposed to automatically improve software's performance, whether through compiler optimisation, parameter tuning, genetic improvement, or other, few consider the interplay between the different non-functional properties [8]. Such automated tooling is needed, given that changes that improve one non-functional property might negatively influence another.

Improving the speed of a program may have unintended consequences. A popular strategy would be caching of intermediate computation results, e.g., in array structures. This, however, leads to increased memory use. Furthermore, if arrays are large enough, the time cost of array operations might outweigh the computational time savings. It is thus important that we consider memory usage when optimising the execution time of an application. In fact finding more memory efficient versions of software can be beneficial to it's speed by saving expensive garbage collection and page swapping operations.

© The Author(s), under exclusive license to Springer Nature Switzerland AG 2022
M. Papadakis and S. R. Vergilio (Eds.): SSBSE 2022, LNCS 13711, pp. 111–117, 2022.
https://doi.org/10.1007/978-3-031-21251-2_8

Although multi-objective search algorithms seem best fit for this problem domain, to the best of our knowledge, there is no tool available that provides this facility, despite such work being proposed in the past [13].

With this in mind, we extended an existing Genetic Improvement (GI) [11] framework, Gin [4], with a multi-objective search strategy[1], namely NSGA-II [6]. We chose GI as it is an approach which can be applied to any source code without the need for tuning or domain expertise. GI utilises search algorithms to find patches which can improve the program with respect to a given objective. GI has already been successfully used to fix bugs, optimise program's runtime, memory, energy consumption, and other [11]. GI has the advantage of being ambivalent to the particular search algorithm used to explore the landscape of patches, thus we can very easily plug in multi-objective algorithms to improve both memory and execution simultaneously or find good trade-offs between them.

To show usefulness of our implementation we target a large, popular, mature piece of software—EvoSuite [7], a tool which utilises Genetic Programming in an attempt to automatically generate test suites for Java programs. EvoSuite then generates and minimises a set of assertions for each test. This allows the tests to detect regressions in future versions of software. EvoSuite is often run with a time limit for test generation for each target class. Once time limit is reached, EvoSuite stops, regardless of whether a particular coverage objective was achieved. It is thus important that EvoSuite can efficiently explore the search landscape, and evaluate generated tests. By improving the speed of EvoSuite we can increase the amount of test cases it can generate and evaluate in the given time limit. At the same time we don't want such improvements to happen at the cost of unnecessary memory use.

Our results are encouraging. We report improvements of up to 78% in runtime and 9% in memory use for 10 methods in EvoSuite software. The best patches removed redundant yet expensive checks, and change the scope of try catch statements. We hope that researchers and practitioners alike find these results encouraging, to apply multi-objective GI to other software, and continue research in this direction. There is more to be explored: which multi-objective algorithms are best fit for search-based software improvement? which other properties could we target? and other. We release our code [1] to facilitate future work.

2 Background

Genetic Improvement uses automated search to improve existing software [11]. GI takes a section of source code and the tests which cover it and searches through a landscape of potential patches in order to find those which improve a given software property. Standard GI operators delete, replace, or copy code fragments, such as statements or lines. Testing is also used as standard as a proxy for capturing software's functional correctness, and to measure the software improvement property of interest. For instance, for runtime improvement, fitness measure of a given program variant will be the time taken by the given test suite.

---

[1] A pull request can be found at https://github.com/gintool/gin/pull/89.

The most popular search algorithm for GI has been genetic programming, however, local search has been recently shown to be as effective [3]. Although White et al. [12] were the first to propose multi-objective (MO) search to improve software's non-functional behaviour, they evolved full programs rather then patches making their approach only applicable to toy software. Basios et al. [2]'s work is closest to what we want to achieve. They used MO to improve memory consumption and runtime of Java applications. However, they used specialised mutations, targeting data structures only. Furthermore, they have not made their code available. This leaves the question of how effective standard GI operators are at MO optimisation unanswered.

3 Approach

We pose that *multi-objective (MO) Genetic Improvement (GI) provides a useful generalist approach for automated software optimisation.*

In order to prove this statement we incorporate multi-objective search into an existing GI framework. We target improvement of non-functional software behaviour, as it's been shown that changes that improve such properties are often non-obvious and their impact on other software properties is hard to predict [5]. We also aim to improve a large, mature piece of code, that comes with an extensive (99% line coverage) test suite. Given the effort put into development of such a piece of software, we expect it will be challenging to find improvements. Thus, if any are found, it will provide strong evidence for usefulness of multi-objective GI.

4 Methodology

In our empirical study we use an existing GI tool, and extend it with a multi-objective algorithm, namely, NSGA-II [6], as it's one of the most popular MO algorithms and proved successful in previous related work [2]. Otherwise, we use the most common GI settings. In particular, we mutate statements, and use 4 standard GI mutation operators, as the building blocks for our generated patches. Each can either *delete* a statement, *copy* one statement from one location to another, *replace* a statement with another, or *swap* locations of two statements. Moreover, we set each run of GI to consists of 40 individuals and 10 generations, for a total of 400 evaluations as shown to be effective in previous GI work [10]. We repeat each GI run 10 times, to account for the non-deterministic nature of NSGA-II. We also separately evaluate each patch found 20 times, to account for noise in fitness measure, as it's often encountered when measuring non-functional properties of software.

GI Tool. Recent survey of GI tooling, revealed that [13] few GI tools can be easily applied to unseen software. After closer investigation we chose Gin [4], as it is the only one to implement fitness functions for at least two non-functional software properties, namely runtime and memory consumption. Moreover, it provides profilers for both properties, thus helps automatically identify the most time and memory consuming parts of code. Runtime fitness measure takes the elapsed time on a set of tests. Memory fitness measure simply calculates memory use before and after a test is run.

Target Software. As our target software we chose EvoSuite—a tool for automatic test generation. It has 1.1 million lines of code, it's been developed for 11 years, and comes with an extensive test suite. We ran Gin's memory and runtime profilers on the evosuite-client module, which contains the code for actual test generation. The profilers' output provides us with a list of methods with the largest impact on memory and execution time, along with the tests that cover those methods. Unfortunately, at this point we discovered a bug in Gin's test runners. EvoSuite uses an example project in a different package for many of it's tests and these tests are not compatible with Gin, we chose to discard the methods covered by these tests and focus on those which had all passing tests. This resulted in 27 methods from the execution time profiler and one method from the memory profiler. We further filtered out methods with less than 5 lines of code as they would be too small for improvements to be found. From here we selected the method found by the memory profiler and the top 9 slowest methods with more than 5 lines of code, giving us 10 methods to attempt to improve. The line coverage of the tests on each method can be found in Table 1.

5 Results and Discussion

In this section we present the improvements which we found to EvoSuite using our multi-objective genetic improvement approach.

Table 1. Table showing execution time improvements found by GI. Numbers in brackets indicate the effect the patch had on the other property, i.e., memory use.

Method	Execution time imp.		Line coverage
	Median	Max	
MersenneTwister.nextGaussian	55.84%	67.12% (−1.1%)	100%
TestFactory.addConstructor	34.9%	37.98% (−2.13%)	73%
RegexDistanceUtils.cacheRegex	12.83%	30.29% (−0.53%)	100%
DistanceCalculator.visit	27.88%	60.62% (−0.81%)	84%
FileIOUtils.recursiveCopy	0.39%	0.42% (−2.33%)	100%
TestCodeVisitor.visitPrimitiveStatement	42.42%	44.44% (−1.02%)	80%
DistanceEstimator.getDistance	48.62%	49.86% (−6.28%)	87%
TestCodeVisitor.getClassName	67.54%	78.77% (−7.05%)	85%
DistanceCalculator.getStringDistance	22.46%	25.63% (−0.67%)	70%
StringHelper.StringRegionMatches	51.91%	58.28% (−2.9%)	80%

Over our 10 runs we find improvements for every single method which we tried to improve, with improvements to runtime of up to 78.8% and improvements to memory of up to 9.2% (see Table 1, and our repository for all Pareto Fronts [1]). Interestingly, the method highlighted by Gin's memory profiler was the only method in which we could

Table 2. Table showing memory improvements found by GI. Numbers in brackets indicate the effect the patch had on the other property, i.e., runtime.

Method	Memory imp.	
	Median	Max
DistanceEstimator.getDistance	2.72%	5.81% (20.49%)
DistanceCalculator.visit	2.73%	4.43% (9.96%)
TestFactory.addConstructor	2.51%	4.12% (18.83%)
StringHelper.StringRegionMatches	2.04%	3.64% (17.49%)
MersenneTwister.nextGaussian	1.64%	4.58% (−4.89%)
TestCodeVisitor.getClassName	3.37%	9.2% (1.89%)
RegexDistanceUtils.cacheRegex	2.49%	8.46% (−7.44%)
FileIOUtils.recursiveCopy	0.00%	0.00% (−0.23%)
DistanceCalculator.getStringDistance	6.52%	6.76% (−12.85%)
TestCodeVisitor.visitPrimitiveStatement	4.3%	5.76% (11.37%)

not find any improvements to memory. The method in question copies files from one place to another, in doing so it loads the contents of the files being copied into memory 2048 bytes at a time. Perhaps reducing the size of this buffer would reduce the memory usage, at the cost of execution time, but our mutation operators are not able to make this kind of change. Using mutation operators which modify constants could lead to further improvements.

We find that, in all cases, the best improvements to execution time lead to memory usage increasing, mostly by small amounts. However, in one case, it increased by almost 6%. Improvements to memory lead to improvements to execution time in 6 cases. This could be due to fewer GC calls. In 4 cases, the best memory improvements also lead to an increase in execution time. These patches offer developers a choice over which property is more important to them, and could also allow multiple versions of EvoSuite to be made available to systems with different hardware resources.

A patch to the TestCodeVisitor.getClassName method was one which improved execution time the most, finding an improvement of almost 80%, on the example EvoSuite class called Tutorial_Stack. This patch leads to a 4.8% improvement on the number of generations evaluated. It is made up of 3 edits, 1 delete, 1 copy, and 1 replace statement edits. The main execution time improvement from the patch comes from removing a conditional which checks whether or not the current ClassLoader for the system under test has the class and then gets the class's Canonical. The area of code which is removed is wrapped in a try catch which ignores exceptions and is able to fail without consequence on the rest of the method. The code is also accompanied by a comment which states that the code is irrelevant in normal use of EvoSuite and only triggered during testing.

We also find a patch to the TestCodeVisitor.getClassName method that provides the greatest memory consumption reduction. This patch changes the scope of try statement which changes the way in which Java releases resources, thus decreasing memory usage by a small amount. Many memory improvements, however, offer marginally improved speed for slightly improved memory. This may be preferable to the much faster but more memory intensive patches also produced.

All patches (see Table 1 and 2) were subsequently run on the whole EvoSuite test suite, showing no regression errors.

Cost of Genetic Improvement. Each run improving all 10 methods took a median time of 48 min, with the slowest run taking 75 min and the quickest taking only 23 min. The difference between runs is due to the number of compiling patches generated. Runs in which a large number of patches fail to compile will need to run significantly fewer tests and thus complete quicker. We believe this is a relatively small cost for the improvements we found.

6 Conclusion

We extended an existing GI tool to provide the first open source multi-objective genetic improvement tool for Java [1], that can improve software's runtime and memory consumption out-of-the-box. We applied it to the EvoSuite test generation tool. We found improvements to both execution time for all methods improved and memory to all but one of the methods which we improved. We found that the NSGA-II algorithm was able to effectively explore the search landscape of patches, finding good trade-offs between memory and execution. Our approach was relatively fast and fully automatic, requiring no domain expertise.

Acknowlegements. This work was funded by the EPSRC grant EP/P023991/1.

References

1. https://github.com/SOLAR-group/EvoSuiteGI
2. Basios, M., Li, L., Wu, F., Kanthan, L., Barr, E.T.: Darwinian data structure selection. In: ESEC/SIGSOFT FSE, pp. 118–128. ACM (2018)
3. Blot, A., Petke, J.: Empirical comparison of search heuristics for genetic improvement of software. IEEE TEVC **25**(5), 1001–1011 (2021)
4. Brownlee, A.E.I., Petke, J., Alexander, B., Barr, E.T., Wagner, M., White, D.R.: Gin: genetic improvement research made easy. In: Auger, A., Stützle, T. (eds.) GECCO, pp. 985–993. ACM (2019)
5. Bruce, B.R., Petke, J., Harman, M., Barr, E.T.: Approximate oracles and synergy in software energy search spaces. IEEE TSE **45**(11), 1150–1169 (2019)
6. Deb, K., Agrawal, S., Pratap, A., Meyarivan, T.: A fast elitist non-dominated sorting genetic algorithm for multi-objective optimization: NSGA-II. In: Schoenauer, M., et al. (eds.) PPSN 2000. LNCS, vol. 1917, pp. 849–858. Springer, Heidelberg (2000). https://doi.org/10.1007/3-540-45356-3_83
7. Fraser, G., Arcuri, A.: EvoSuite: automatic test suite generation for object-oriented software. In: SIGSOFT FSE, pp. 416–419. ACM (2011)
8. Hort, M., Kechagia, M., Sarro, F., Harman, M.: A survey of performance optimization for mobile applications. IEEE TSE **48**(8), 2879–2904 (2022)

9. Jin, G., Song, L., Shi, X., Scherpelz, J., Lu, S.: Understanding and detecting real-world performance bugs. In: PLDI, PLDI 2012, pp. 77–88 (2012)
10. Motwani, M., Soto, M., Brun, Y., Just, R., Goues, C.L.: Quality of automated program repair on real-world defects. IEEE TSE **48**(2), 637–661 (2022)
11. Petke, J., Haraldsson, S.O., Harman, M., Langdon, W.B., White, D.R., Woodward, J.R.: Genetic improvement of software: a comprehensive survey. IEEE TEVC **22**(3), 415–432 (2018)
12. White, D.R., Arcuri, A., Clark, J.A.: Evolutionary improvement of programs. IEEE TEVC **15**(4), 515–538 (2011)
13. Zuo, S., Blot, A., Petke, J.: Evaluation of genetic improvement tools for improvement of non-functional properties of software. In: Fieldsend, J.E., Wagner, M. (eds.) GECCO 2022, pp. 1956–1965. ACM (2022)

Author Index

Printed in the United States
by Baker & Taylor Publisher Services